Experience Effects in International Investment and Technology Transfer

Research for Business Decisions, No. 34

Gunter Dufey, Series Editor
Professor of International Business and Finance
The University of Michigan

Other Titles in This Series

Experience Effects in International Investment and Technology Transfer

by
William H. Davidson

RESEARCH PRESS

text first submitted as a
typescript facsimile in 1979

Produced and distributed by
UMI Research Press
an imprint of
University Microfilms International
Ann Arbor, Michigan 48106

Library of Congress Cataloging in Publication Data

Davidson, William Harley, 1951-
    Experience effects in international investment
and technology transfer.

    (Research for business decisions ; 34)
    Includes bibliographical references and index.
    1. Investments, American. 2. Foreign licensing
agreements. 3. New products. 4. Technology transfer.
I. Title. II. Series.

HG4538.D29 1981   332.6'7314   80-39884
ISBN 0-8357-1148-X

Contents

List of Figures

List of Figures

List of Tables

Preface

This study is based upon analysis of a sample of 954 commercially and technically significant new products introduced in the United States between 1945-76. These products and the resulting data base are described in Appendix II. Patterns of international manufacturing for this sample of products are used to analyze determinants of foreign investment and licensing activity.

Tests relating experience variables to patterns of foreign manfuacturing are presented in Chapter II. Chapter II focuses on the role of experience effects in location, timing, and recipient decisions.

Chapter III examines how characteristics of the firm encourage or inhibit the realization of experience effects in foreign manufacturing projects. The hypotheses to be tested in that chapter focus on how experience resources are accumulated and applied to individual decisions within an organization.

Chapter IV poses an alternative hypothesis. Acceleration in the international spread of manufacturing can be related to growth of competition in world markets as well as rising corporate experience. Competition is measured by examining levels of technological leads associated with individual products. Analysis of investment patterns for high-technology products suggests that firms do not always pursue "defensive" patterns of foreign investment.

Chapter V explores factors that lead the firm to be more aggressive in initiating foreign production. The effects of experience, uncertainty, and corporate strategy on such decisions are developed.

Chapter VI relates the experience factor to existing theories of foreign investment. The role of experience is incorporated into these models. The implications of the findings of this study for corporate and public policy are also outlined.

Acknowledgments

This study was conducted under the umbrella of the Harvard Multinational Enterprise Project. The support, encouragement, and criticism of Professor Raymond Vernon, the Project Director, provided essential contributions and guidance to the undertaking.

Preparation of the data banks used in this study was funded by the Ford Foundation, the Division of Research at Harvard Business School and the National Science Foundation's Division of Policy Research and Analysis. Compilation of the data was accomplished by a team of more than 30 Harvard undergraduate and graduate students including Nathan Fagre, Lawrence Goodstein, Regina Pisa, and Laurence Ronan. The design and construction of all data bases were handled by Gregory Hammett and Rajan Suri. In addition to these two gentlemen, analytical programming was performed by Gyuri Karody, Teymour Boutros-Ghali, and Peter Gennis.

Professors Raymond Vernon, Louis T. Wells, and Michel Y. Yoshino provided essential assistance in helping to define and structure the issues, concepts, and presentation of this analysis.

The speed and efficiency of Mrs. Suzanne Sweet in preparing the many drafts of the manuscript were greatly appreciated.

Finally, the patience and tolerance of my wife Anneke deserve praise. She was a strong source of support throughout the process of completing this manuscript.

My appreciation and gratitude are extended to all of these people.

Chapter I

International Investment and Technology Transfer

This is a study of foreign direct investment and licensing activity by U.S.-based companies. These activities are important for many reasons, but of principal concern here is their role as the primary channels for international technology transfer. The international spread of U.S. technology through international investment and licensing is the focus of this study. The transfer of technology is measured by tracing the spread of foreign manufacturing for products developed in the United States.

This process warrants interest from three perspectives. First, decisions to manufacture products abroad leave an important impact on corporate performance. Second, these decisions affect areas of significant public policy concern. Third, there appears to be a gap in existing theories of international production. The need for revised approaches to international production theory has been cited by Vernon, Dunning, Parry, and Giddy, among others.[1]

This study attempts to increase understanding of these activities by examining foreign manufacturing histories for a sample of product lines and individual products introduced in the United States since 1945. The analysis focuses on three basic decisions: the *location, timing,* and use of independent licensees, joint ventures or wholly-owned subsidiaries as *recipients* of foreign manufacturing for a product. By focusing on these decisions, it is hoped that more understanding of the determinants of foreign manufacturing activity can be gained. The findings of this study would then be useful in a normative sense to managers, as input to concerned public policymakers, and as a contribution to international production theory.

In examining these activities, a number of basic questions emerge. Why do U.S.-based firms manufacture their products abroad in the first place? Where, when, and how is foreign manufacturing initiated? What factors determine these decisions?

A great deal of existing knowledge can be applied to these questions. The foundation for this analysis derives from two related fields of study. The first area comprises a set of theories pertaining to international trade and investment. The second can be thought of as encompassing studies of the international spread of technology. This study overlaps both areas.

The principal focal point in this analysis is the effect of experience factors on international investment and licensing patterns. Various measures of experience are employed to reflect the scale economies, learning benefits, and uncertainty reduction that accumulate within the firm in the course of foreign activity. Tests of the relationship of these variables to location, timing, and recipient patterns suggest they play a significant role in these decisions.

This study is concerned with only one facet of foreign direct investment activity. When such activity is measured in terms of observations based on product lines, as in this study, two major types of investment can be distinguished. One is the acquisition of existing foreign product lines, and the second is the establishment of a firm's existing product in foreign markets.[2] These existing products, with rare exception for U.S.-based multinationals, originate in the United States. As shall be seen, this second type of activity, the focus of this study, has assumed increasing importance in recent years.

A second distinction is important. In examining the foreign spread of manufacturing for U.S. products, two types of activity can be distinguished. One type of investment, best represented by U.S.-owned plants in Taiwan and the Mexican border-zone, is designed to manufacture components or assemble finished products for export. The second type of plant is designed to serve primarily the market in which it is located. This second type of manufacturing activity is emphasized in this study. The vast majority of foreign manufacturing subsidiaries serve primarily the market in which they are located. Data on 3,830 foreign manufacturing subsidiaries reveal that only 9.5 percent of these subsidiaries exported more than 50 percent of their sales in 1975.[3]

Why do the bulk of foreign manufacturing subsidiaries focus almost entirely on their local markets? Tariffs and transport costs are important, but a more powerful force is at work here. Two immediate reasons relate to the firm's desire to reduce risk. By manufacturing in the foreign market, two types of risk are eliminated. Production within the market means that manufacturing costs and sales revenue are denominated in the same currency, thus avoiding uncertainty associated with currency and price fluctuations.[4] Second, by manufacturing in the foreign market certain political uncertainties are reduced. Host governments can restrict imports at any time, and such actions often result when a competitor intitiates manufacturing within the foreign market. The risk of losing a market through such actions declines when a product is manufactured within the market, although the firm incurs additional risk of another variety by investing in the foreign nation. Relations with host governments are a key factor in production location decisions. Before exploring this issue further, however, a more basic view of foreign manufacturing decisions should be considered.

A number of models can be employed to explain patterns of foreign manufacturing activity. Operations research techniques apply to foreign manufacturing decisions. Such location models attempt to identify least-cost locations for manufacturing activity. In such models, linear programming is used to account for tariff and transport costs, factor costs, scale economies, and the location of markets.[5] Other factors, such as tax rates, subsidies, and grants could also be included in these models. Political risk factors would be more difficult to incorporate. In any event, such models apply primarily to export plant location decisions. A different framework is needed for the vast majority of foreign manufacturing facilities which are intended to serve a single market.

The key variable in decisions to produce within an individual foreign market is timing. A normative model can be developed to structure such decisions.

The firm maximizes profit by serving the foreign market via exports until sales volume warrants foreign production. At point Q in Figure 1-1, the cost of serving the market via export equals the cost of serving it via manufacturing within the market. At volumes in excess of Q, production facilities within the market will be more efficient than exports.

Figure 1-1
Comparison of Sourcing Alternatives for a Foreign Market:
Cost of Export and Local Production Strategies

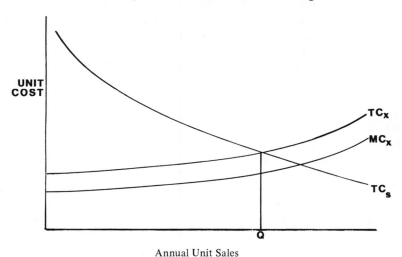

Annual Unit Sales
Volume in the Foreign Market

MC_X = Marginal Unit Cost of Manufacturing in an Existing Plant and Exporting to the Market

TC_X = Total Unit Cost of Serving Market via Exports
(${MC_X}$ Plus Tariff and Transport costs).

TC_S = Total Unit Cost of Manufacturing within the Market.

In order to structure this decision, numerous assumptions are needed. This framework assumes that the relationship between exchange rates and variable production costs in the two countries remains constant. Tariff and transport costs must also be assumed constant. Real capital costs associated with the foreign plant are assumed to remain constant over the period. In addition, it is assumed that once annual volume exceeds Q in any year, it will continue to do so over the estimated life of the project. With such assumptions, the firm maximizes profit by bringing a plant on stream in the market for the first year in which local volume exceeds Q.

Once volume warrants foreign production, a second issue arises. Under classical theory, foreign manufacturing would not be realized through the mechanism of direct investment. Foreign direct investment can only occur if a U.S. firm, in this case, values the foreign investment project more highly than any firm in the foreign country. Explanation of how such divergences in valuation result is the objective of any theory of foreign investment.

Existing theories of foreign investment explain the existence of divergences in valuation in several ways. Theories of foreign investment can be categorized into two broad groups. Theories in each group share a common assumption that market imperfections motivate foreign direct investment, but they differ as to the nature and relative importance of these imperfections. One set of theories emphasizes financial considerations as the motive for foreign direct investment; the second focuses on oligopoly factors as determinants of foreign investment activity.

The financial theories are best represented by Aliber's theory of currency premiums[6] and the work of Grubel, Lessard, Solnik, and Rugman[7] on the benefits of international diversification. Aliber's theory holds that U.S.-based firms place a higher value on foreign cash flows than existing financial markets in foreign countries. This holds because U.S. firms have lower discount rates, a function of their lower costs of capital. These lower capital costs derive from international lenders' desire to hold dollar debt and investors' desire to hold dollar-denominated securities. The result is a "currency premium" which acts to encourage foreign direct investment by U.S.-based firms. Because of this effect, U.S. firms value foreign cash flows more highly than foreign firms. When returns in foreign markets exceed those to be derived from comparable U.S. investments, the result is direct investment abroad.

In one respect, lower capital costs encourage foreign investment in a manner similar to the way in which premium price-earnings ratios encourage conglomerate acquisitions in the domestic U.S. financial market. Financial markets value a profit stream held by U.S. firms more than if it were held by a foreign firm. Conglomerate acquisition activity has subsided as P-E ratios for such firms have declined, and, similarly, recent trends in international P-E ratios raise questions about the role of currency premiums in U.S. direct investment activity.[8] Another set of finance-based theories has begun to fill this gap.

In the view of many, the benefits of diversification established by Markowitz[9] extend to international investment. The firm is willing to pay a premium for foreign cash flows because, on a risk-adjusted basis, they enhance the value of the firm.[10] In this model, foreign cash flows again are valued more highly by U.S. firms than by the local financial market, encouraging foreign investment.

As outgrowths of finance and portfolio theory, these models are perhaps most applicable to international portfolio investment. In terms of direct investment, they hold more relevance to acquisition activity than to the introduction of U.S. product lines abroad. When the issue of manufacturing a product abroad is considered, there are a number of other factors which are likely to have far more impact on valuation of the project than cost of capital differentials. For example, operating efficiencies are likely to vary substantially among potential investors in a start-up situation for a new product, whereas this factor is not as significant in an acquisition. Such factors are likely to have far more impact on valuations of the project than currency premiums or portfolio benefits.

Inter-firm differences in production costs or imperfections in markets for inputs to a project can have a very important effect on decisions to produce abroad. The oligopoly-based models develop the sources and effects of such market imperfections.

Hymer[11] states that foreign direct investment can occur only if the firm possesses competitive advantages which outweigh the additional costs associated with doing business in a distant foreign nation. The sources of such competitive advantage are diverse. Caves emphasizes the role of differentiated brand names and marketing strength.[12] Vernon focuses on the role of technology in international investment.[13] Scale economies, management resources, information, government support, and control of markets also convey competitive advantages. These factors provide the cost advantages and strategic strengths which promote foreign investment.

These oligopoly factors serve as barriers to entry that inhibit foreign firms from initiating manufacturing for a product. These barriers can be surmounted, however, most notably through licensing arrangements. If foreign firms value a project more highly than the U.S. firm controlling the product line, licensing would benefit both firms. For example, assume that a foreign firm's estimate of the net present value for a project exceeds that of the U.S. firm. This firm requires access to proprietary inputs to pursue the project, however. Any net present value payment for a license that falls between the foreign and U.S. firms' valuations of the project will benefit both parties, assuming opportunity costs are accounted for in the original valuations.

Since foreign firms possess significant cost advantages associated with operating in their own market, it can be argued that all foreign manufacturing could be initiated more efficiently through licensing agreements. This point can be refuted by economic analysis. The host country firm's market-specific overheads will not be fully transferable to all projects, and such firms will not possess the product-specific overheads and efficiencies generated by the U.S. firm. A project can provide external benefits or scale economies to a U.S. firm that cannot be realized by a foreign firm. The U.S. firm may have slack managerial and other resources, for example. Chandler established the role of this factor in diversification,[14] and Dubin extended the relationship to foreign direct investment.[15] A key issue in this regard, of course, is the transferability of such resources to a foreign environment.

Inefficiencies in markets for proprietary inputs also inhibit licensing and stimulate direct investment. Buckley and Casson argue that firms invest abroad because they cannot realize the highest returns on proprietary brand names, technology, or knowledge through direct sale of such assets to foreign parties.[16] Arrow has shown that the market value of information may be discounted because of buyer uncertainty.[17] As a result of such uncertainty, the firm can frequently realize higher returns through direct investment.

It is important to consider, however, that the U.S. firm will also be affected by uncertainty. The firm may be highly uncertain about operating in a foreign market. When the firm is uncertain about a foreign project, it will discount the value of that project. The phenomena of discounting the value of an uncertain outcome is well established in utility and preference theory.[18] This will encourage licensing activity, but also will lead the firm to serve foreign markets via export longer than economics justify.

Such behavior is implicit in the product cycle model.[19] Under this paradigm, the shift from export to foreign production generally occurs not as a result of favorable analysis of production costs, but in response to a competitive or political threat in the foreign market. Such "defensive" behavior is a function of the firm's ability to ignore the dictates of the market because of its market power, and its desire to do so because of high uncertainty levels associated with foreign production.

There are many sources of this uncertainty. Political risk, uncertain wage and productivity levels and raw material costs, possibilities of quality control problems, uncertainty about market trends or currency rates, and concern for industry stability all may deter foreign production. Regardless of its sources, this uncertainty contributes to a defensive approach to foreign production. As a result, firms will postpone foreign production beyond volumes calculated as break-even levels.

It is important to distinguish between uncertainty and risk in this regard. Foreign investment decisions are marked by high degrees of uncertainty, in the Knightian sense.[20] The variables and dimensions of risk affecting the outcome of such projects are simply not known by the decision-maker.

Uncertainty and Experience

Uncertainty, and the firm's aversion to it, are difficult to measure. However, much can be learned by testing the effects of experience on comparable decisions. If firms postpone foreign manufacturing because of high levels of uncertainty, as posed in the product cycle model, reductions in uncertainty levels should result in lower decision thresholds for foreign production projects.

Uncertainty levels will decline as the firm becomes more familiar with international operations in general and in individual markets. This reduction will affect decisions to produce abroad. Vernon has stated that the product cycle paradigm:

> may be an efficient way to look at enterprises that are on the threshold of developing a foreign business, but the model is losing some of its relevance for enterprises that have long since acquired a global economic capacity and a global habit of mind.[21]

L.T. Wells, in the introduction to *The Product Life Cycle and International Trade,* also has commented that:

> the product life cycle offers food for thought as to what the effect of the spread of multinational enterprises might be. With the establishment of efficient information networks among subsidiaries, the gap between introduction in the first market and a second market might be diminished.[22]

The defensive model of initiating foreign production may be particularly relevant to cases of initial manufacturing investment in a foreign country. Such cases are characterized by a high degree of uncertainty. However, it is important to recognize that such uncertainty will decline for subsequent investments. This can affect the timing and level of direct investment.

Experience will also affect location patterns of foreign investment. One can hypothesize that firms will prefer to manufacture in nations where they have existing subsidiaries. This is true for several reasons. Existing subsidiaries have already incurred the start-up costs associated with entering a foreign market. Certain overhead costs will be absorbed by existing operations.

The presence of an existing facility reduces the total costs associated with foreign production. The lower cost curve for production in an existing subsidiary implies that firms will shift to foreign production from export more quickly in markets where they have existing facilities, as presented in Figure 1-2. In addition to static scale economies, there may also be learning benefits associated with manufacturing in an established subsidiary. Trained management and technicians are already present in the foreign subsidiary. Experience in transfer of product technology will reduce costs associated with initiation of foreign production.

Figure 1-2
**Comparison of Sourcing Alternatives for a Foreign Market:
Cost of Export, Production in an Existing Subsidiary
and Production in a New Subsidiary**

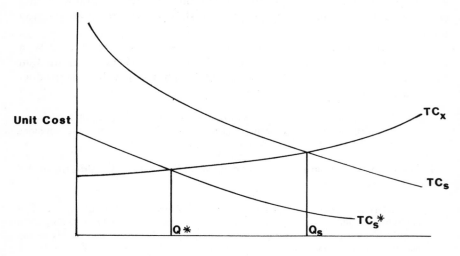

Annual Sales Volume
in the Foreign Market

TC_X = Total Unit Cost of Export

TC_S = Total Unit Cost in a New Subsidiary

TC_S^* = Total Cost to U.S. Firm in an Existing Subsidiary

     Risk and uncertainty are again important in this decision. The firm may include a risk premium in its calculations of foreign production cost. This premium may be less for established subsidiaries than for potential new ones, since the firm has less uncertainty about productivity and wage levels, supply of inputs, quality control, and political climate.

     These three elements, scale economies, learning benefits, and reduced uncertainty, constitute the experience factor. The term experience factor is frequently associated with the effects of the learning curve phenomenon on manufacturing costs. As used here, the experience factor refers to a broader set of benefits. The learning curve reflects cost reductions achieved through repetition of tasks; its principal focus falls on the area of manufacturing. Experience effects reflect not only learning benefits in manufacturing, but also learning benefits in other functional and administrative areas. Experience effects also include static scale economies derived from the use of physical facilities and organizational systems. Organizational scale economies, achieved in the use of administrative systems and personnel, are an important element in the experience factor. Uncertainty reduction, or the accumulation of information, also represents an important organizational element in the experience factor. Where the learning curve focuses on volume as the principal determinant of competitiveness, the experience factor emphasizes the importance of functional and administrative economies and information at both central and foreign locations.

These experience effects will have a significant impact on foreign investment and licensing patterns. A number of specific results can be suggested.

1. Increased experience will result in more rapid and extensive manufacturing activity in foreign subsidiaries.
2. Increased experience will result in lower rates of licensing in initiating foreign manufacturing.

A number of corollaries can also be suggested. It can be hypothesized that firms will prefer nations in which they operate an existing subsidiary over other nations as foreign manufacturing sites, ceteris paribus. This will be reflected by more rapid and extensive activity in such countries. These effects will build on themselves, in that increased experience stimulates foreign manufacturing, and foreign activity contributes to experience. Consequently, these trends can be expected to accelerate over time.

Chapter II

The Experience Factor

The immediate postwar world provided an environment uniquely favorable to the expansion of international trade and investment. This environment was particularly favorable for firms based in the United States. Barriers to trade and investment were eliminated or reduced through the actions of GATT and the IMF, through destruction of prewar cartels and through public commitments to growth and a progressive global economic order. U.S. industry, faced with a competitive vacuum in many foreign markets, expanded abroad at a rapid rate.

United States industry used several different means of serving foreign demand for their products. Exports of manufactured goods from the U.S. grew from under $10 billion in 1950 to over $80 billion in 1977.[1] Exports as a percentage of GNP almost doubled during this period.

Exports from the U.S. have not been the principal channel for serving foreign markets, however. Foreign manufacturing accounts for the bulk of U.S. sales abroad. Sales of majority-owned foreign manufacturing affiliates grew from under $5 billion in 1950 to over $200 billion in 1977.[2]

Licensing activity has also increased dramatically. United States royalty receipts provide one measure of licensing activity. Receipts from nonaffiliated foreign firms grew from under $50 million in 1950 to $760 million in 1975. It is important to note that royalty receipts from affiliates, a by-product of direct investment activity, have grown far more rapidly to over $3.5 billion in 1975.[3]

These aggregated data suggest that foreign direct investment has served as the principal channel for initiating manufacturing in foreign markets. The following section focuses on direct investment activity alone.

Patterns of Foreign Direct Investment 1945-75

The Harvard Multinational Enterprise Project surveyed the activities of 180 large U.S.-based multinational enterprises through 1975. These 180 firms represent an estimated 70 percent of total U.S. foreign direct investment in manufacturing as of 1975. Consequently, these data present a very large sample for analysis of direct investment activity. The sample is biased in two respects, however. The 180 firms in the sample were selected from the 1965 Fortune 500 if they owned manufacturing plants in six or more nations. Firms that have developed overseas manufacturing networks since that time are not represented in the sample. Because of reliance on the Fortune 500, smaller firms are also not represented. Despite these limitations, the sample provides an extensive view of U.S. direct investment activity.

The most obvious pattern emerging from the data is the rapid growth of foreign manufacturing networks since 1945. These 180 firms acquired or formed over 7,000 foreign manufacturing subsidiaries between 1945 and 1976. The rate of new subsidiary entries rose dramatically until peaking in 1970. The number of new entries in the 1971-75 period, although lower than the 1966-70 period, still exceeds that of any prior period.

TABLE 2-1

Foreign Manufacturing Subsidiaries
Established by 180 U.S.-based Multinational
Enterprises: By Period of Entry

Number of Subsidiary Entries	Period of Entry							
	Pre-1946	1946-1950	1951-1955	1956-1960	1961-1965	1966-1970	1971-1975	Total
Number of Entries	748	225	409	940	1,594	2,184	1,856	7,756
Entry Method								
Acquired	230	41	181	486	844	1,344	1,126	4,252
Newly Formed	481	161	202	413	664	791	702	3,214
Unknown	37	23	26	41	86	49	28	290

It is notable that the use of acquisitions has increased during this period of dramatic foreign expansion. This trend may reflect a general scarcity of international management resources within U.S.-based firms. The creation of newly-formed subsidiaries requires far more management than the acquisition of a going concern with an existing management team. Dubin has stated that the desire to secure existing management resources is a prime motive behind international acquisition activity.[4]

New subsidiary entries serve as one measure of foreign direct investment activity. It is important to note that this measure neglects a significant aspect of foreign direct investment activity—the introduction of new product lines into existing subsidiaries. An indication of the magnitude of this type of activity can be gained by examining data on the product lines manufactured within individual subsidiaries. Such data appear in Table 2-2.

Product line information was gathered for each of over 7,000 foreign manufacturing subsidiaries in the sample. These product lines are recorded by

TABLE 2-2

SIC 3-Digit Product Lines Manufactured
by the Foreign Subsidiaries of 180 U.S.-based Multinational
Enterprises, by Period and Method of Entry

Method of Entry	Pre-1946	1946-1950	1951-1955	1956-1960	1961-1965	1966-1970	1971-1975	Total
Total Number of Product Line Entries	907	262	528	1,181	1,965	4,564	3,784	13,191
% Entering by Acquisition of Established Foreign Firms	27.9	23.3	36.0	42.3	47.4	37.7	35.0	37.8
% Entering in Newly-Formed Subsidiaries	69.0	68.0	55.3	49.1	44.6	24.0	20.9	33.5
% Entering into Existing Subsidiaries	3.1	8.7	8.7	8.6	8.0	38.3	44.1	28.7

SIC 3-digit classifications. By examining patterns of expansion in these product line observations, a more comprehensive picture of foreign direct investment activity can be gained.

These product line data reveal an important trend. The introduction of new product lines into existing subsidiaries has risen dramatically in recent years. This type of expansion also conserves management resources and permits realization of scale economies in existing subsidiaries.

Existing foreign subsidiaries provide an important base for further expansion. United States firms have made substantial investments in developing channels of distribution, manufacturing facilities, and local management resources in foreign countries. These resources can be utilized to promote further expansion. They also represent overhead that must be absorbed. Multinational firms utilize the capacity of their established systems to best advantage by introducing additional complementary product lines into existing subsidiaries.

As this study is concerned primarily with the international spread of manufacturing for U.S. products, product line data provide a useful medium for analysis of patterns in foreign manufacturing activity. One variable of prime concern is the location pattern of foreign manufacturing. Where is manufacturing for U.S. product lines initiated?

Location Patterns

A great deal of research has been devoted to this question. Factors such as market size and growth[5] have been used as proxies to reflect the effects of market volume on foreign manufacturing decisions. Political climate[6] and financial restrictions[7] are also considered important determinants of location decisions. Do these factors help explain absolute differences in levels of manufacturing activity for different nations? Examination of Table 2-3 raises several questions. First, why do Canada and the U.K. account for such disproportionate shares of foreign manufacturing activity?

The level of manufacturing activity by U.S.-based firms in Canada and the U.K. exceeds any estimates that could be derived from analysis of market size and growth. Transportation and tariffs are relatively insignificant factors in regard to these two nations, thus encouraging the use of exports to serve the markets. Their currencies have been weak relative to the dollar, discouraging exports, but on a price-adjusted basis, manufacturing costs have risen more rapidly than in the U.S.[8] Perhaps the prime motive for this activity lies elsewhere.

Linder proposed that trade, and consequently investment, occurs primarily between nations with similar tastes and products.[9] As evidence, trade patterns in beverages, packaged food, automobiles, and consumer goods often reveal a two-way flow of similar goods between trading partners.

Table 2-3

SIC 3-Digit Product Lines
Manufactured Abroad By
Subsidiaries of 180 U.S.-based
Multinational Enterprises, by Country
and Period of Entry

Country	Pre-1946	1946-50	1951-55	Period of Entry 1956-60	1961-65	1966-70	1971-75	Total
Total Number	907	262	528	1,181	1,965	4,564	3,784	13,191
Percentage in:								
Mexico	4.9%	11.8%	7.4%	8.7%	6.5%	5.9%	6.1%	6.4%
Brazil	5.0	5.7	6.8	5.3	2.0	3.9	6.4	4.7
Argentina	5.2	3.1	3.4	3.2	3.1	2.9	1.8	2.8
Colombia	2.2	4.2	2.8	2.8	2.7	1.5	1.6	2.0
Other Latin American	7.8	12.6	9.1	10.7	9.2	6.8	5.5	7.5
Canada	24.6	21.4	21.2	11.6	10.2	12.9	11.2	13.2
U.K.	14.7	13.4	8.1	9.7	9.6	10.3	12.1	10.9
W. Germany	5.5	1.9	7.6	5.8	6.3	7.4	7.3	6.8
France	5.6	3.4	4.0	7.1	6.7	5.9	6.5	6.1
Italy	1.9	1.5	2.7	5.2	6.0	4.3	3.9	4.2
Spain	1.8	0.8	2.3	1.5	4.0	3.1	3.6	3.0
Belgium	1.5	1.1	0.9	1.9	2.7	3.8	3.1	2.9
Netherlands	1.3	1.9	0.9	1.9	2.3	2.4	2.4	2.2
Ireland	0.7	1.1	1.3	0.4	0.8	0.8	0.9	0.8
Other European	3.5	2.8	2.8	3.2	4.3	5.3	4.3	4.6
S. Africa	3.7	3.8	2.5	2.5	3.2	2.5	2.3	2.6
Other African	0.0	1.1	0.6	1.5	2.1	2.1	2.0	1.8
Australia	4.9	2.3	5.3	8.5	4.9	6.8	5.8	6.1
Japan	0.6	0.8	3.2	2.1	4.7	3.9	4.6	3.8
India	0.9	1.9	0.8	1.8	1.9	1.2	1.1	1.3
Philippines	1.1	1.5	2.3	1.5	1.0	1.1	0.9	1.1
Taiwan	0.0	0.0	0.3	0.3	0.4	0.6	0.7	0.5
S. Korea	0.0	0.0	0.1	0.2	0.2	0.4	0.5	0.3
Other Asian	2.6	1.9	3.6	2.6	5.2	4.2	5.4	4.4

Vernon offers an extended view of this process.[10] In this view, the development and design of new products are responsive to national economic conditions. In the U.S., affluence and a relative scarcity of labor have stimulated the development of consumer luxury products and labor-saving capital equipment.[11] According to this theory, these innovations tend to appear abroad first in nations with similar market characteristics; those with high per-capita incomes and relatively expensive labor. Consumers in such markets will respond most quickly to products with characteristics designed to meet needs highly similar to their own.

In addition to economic conditions, cultural similarity also plays an important role in stimulating the spread of new products. Information about a new product is more efficiently disseminated in a similar language and culture. Education plays a key role in determining adoption rates for new technologies,[12] and this process is promoted by the absence of cultural or lingual barriers. The firm also achieves greater economies of scale in these similar markets. Existing resources, such as advertising, packaging, design, market research, and manufacturing technology are more readily transferable to such markets.

The ability of the firm to utilize its existing human resources in such markets is also a key factor. These human resources will be highly transferable to similar countries. For more foreign cultures, the firm must hire and develop new human resources. This takes time and requires an investment that discourages manufacturing activity.

As a result of these forces, production will be initiated more often in nations with similar cultural and economic characteristics. This view is consistent with the results in Table 2-3. Canada, the United Kingdom, and Australia account for 30.2% of all U.S. product lines manufactured abroad.

Market size is generally recognized as a principal determinant of location patterns. Market similarity also appears to play an important role. The relative effects of these and other factors on location decisions can be examined by analysis of absolute levels of investment activity. However, an alternative approach offers a better opportunity to examine the effects of various factors on location patterns. This approach, derived from a technique developed by Vaupel,[13] generates country manufacturing sequences for SIC 3-digit product lines in a canonical form matrix.[14]

Country manufacturing sequences were compiled for each SIC 3-digit industry within each of the 180 firms in the sample. For each such "parent-industry," the sequence of investment was arrayed by country. For example, the country investment sequence for one parent in industry 357 appears as follows.

Country Investment Sequence for a Firm in SIC Industry 357

Host Country	Year of Initial Production
Canada	1959
U.K.	1963
France	1964
Mexico	1964
Australia	1969
Japan	1973

Such data were compiled for each parent-industry. From these observations, "entry frequencies" were calculated for a set of 20 major countries. These entry frequencies were calculated by determining the percentage of cases in which manufacturing for a product line was initiated in one country before others.

Frequencies for each country are derived from the formula:

$$F_i = \Sigma F_{ij} = \sum_{k=1}^{N} \frac{A_{ij}}{A_{ij} + A_{ji}} \quad k = \sum_{k=1}^{N} \frac{A_{ijk}}{N}$$

F_{ij} is the observed ratio with which firms established production in country i before country j. The symbol k represents a parent-industry produced in either country i or j; each of these N observations will be assigned to A_{ij} or A_{ji}, depending on whether it appeared first in country i or country j.[15] F_{ij} is calculated by dividing the number of times production was initiated in country i before country j by N, the total number of parent-industries produced in either country.

The resultant matrix of cumulative entry frequencies for 380 country-pairs appears in Table 2-4. For ease of presentation, since F_{ij} plus F_{ji} sums to one, only one frequency for each country-pair is presented in this table.

The countries are listed in descending order of priority in the manufacturing sequence according to aggregate entry frequencies. The last column in the table presents the sum of individual frequencies for each country. Canada is given priority over all other countries in the sequence, both individually and in the aggregate. United States firms initiated manufacturing for SIC 3-digit industries in Canada before the United Kingdom in 59.1 percent of all cases. Manufacturing was initiated in Canada before West Germany in 69.3 percent of all cases, and for all other nations in more than 70 percent of all parent industries.

The location preferences apparent in Table 2-4 suggest the effects of various factors. There is a general correlation between position in the sequence and market size. Rank correlations were conducted to analyze the relationship between market size and position in the sequence. The 20 nations were ranked in terms of average GNP between 1950 and 1975.

There is a strong relationship between market size and position in the manufacturing sequence. This relationship is statistically significant at the level of .01 probability. Market size, even as measured crudely here in absolute GNP terms, appears to serve as a proxy for the production economies and oligopoly factors that determine foreign manufacturing patterns. If production is initiated in a foreign market when warranted by volume, larger markets will reach those volume levels more rapidly, assuming consumers adopt the product at equal rates in different markets. Larger markets also may

Figure 2-1
Twenty Nations by Average GNP Rank for 1950 and 1975
and Position in Manufacturing Sequence

Nation	Rank in GNP	Position in Sequence
West Germany	1	3
France	2	6
United Kingdom	3	2
Japan	4	8
Canada	5	1
Italy	6	10
India	7	15
Spain	8	9
Brazil	9	7
Australia	10	4
Mexico	11	5
Netherlands	12	14
Argentina	13	13
Belgium	14	12
S. Africa	15	16
Philippines	16	17
S. Korea	17	19
Colombia	18	11
Taiwan	19	20
Ireland	20	18

Rank Correlation Coefficient   .791

Probability of Significance   .01

TÄBLÈ 2-4

Frequency by which 180 U.S.-based Multinational Enterprise Initiated
Manufacturing for SIC 3-digit Industries in Country A before
Country B, 1900-76

Country A												Country B									
	2	3	4	5	6	7	8	9	10	11	12	13	14	15	16	17	18	19	20	Total
1. Canada	.591	.693	.737	.740	.744	.782	.784	.826	.839	.853	.853	.892	.916	.884	.909	.976	.984	.986	.994	15.983
2. U. Kingdom		.605	.666	.644	.667	.675	.703	.767	.769	.776	.808	.843	.876	.845	.888	.961	.972	.980	.992	14.846
3. W. Germany			.545	.483	.550	.556	.576	.656	.722	.773	.717	.769	.817	.771	.798	.915	.967	.967	.972	13.256
4. Mexico				.513	.536	.568	.611	.689	.669	.669	.756	.776	.766	.812	.806	.967	.946	.972	.983	13.172
5. Australia					.500	.524	.579	.638	.647	.653	.784	.750	.813	.787	.813	.928	.944	.965	.971	12.794
6. France						.503	.557	.614	.631	.645	.700	.746	.772	.796	.796	.905	.945	.962	.962	12.578
7. Brazil							.552	.621	.612	.631	.678	.741	.748	.762	.802	.936	.949	.955	.974	12.353
8. Japan								.575	.573	.555	.672	.716	.702	.748	.757	.927	.951	.972	.993	11.779
9. Spain									.486	.505	.584	.643	.650	.673	.696	.801	.929	.945	.963	10.489
10. Italy										.515	.575	.638	.610	.617	.689	.872	.906	.941	.967	10.380
11. Colombia											.603	.664	.652	.687	.686	.891	.915	.941	.924	10.371
12. Belgium												.549	.580	.544	.593	.819	.886	.928	.927	9.026
13. Netherlands													.532	.527	.580	.678	.897	.897	.924	8.308
14. S. Africa														.561	.568	.759	.882	.909	.895	8.140
15. Argentina															.537	.789	.877	.903	.903	8.117
16. India																.727	.842	.942	.941	7.534
17. Philippines																	.656	.750	.731	4.286
18. Ireland																		.550	.625	2.727
19. South Korea																			.500	2.005
20. Taiwan																				1.856
																				190.00

stimulate more investment activity than smaller markets if oligopolists are concerned with market share and relative size in the industry.

Despite this high degree of correlation, a casual observation of Figure 2-1 shows some major discrepancies between rank by size and position in the manufacturing sequence. Germany, France, and Japan, three of the largest foreign markets, do not receive a commensurate priority in the manufacturing sequence. These variances suggest that other forces are at work.

Geographic proximity can be cited as a factor that stimulates activity in Canada, Mexico, and Colombia beyond what might be estimated from consideration of market size, for example. The effects of market similarity again appear to be highly significant. Canada and the U.K. receive highest priority in the investment sequence, and Australia is given preference over every other nation except West Germany.

Multivariate tests could be developed to test the relationships between market size, growth, geographic proximity, market similarity, political risk, and investment sequences. That is not the intent of this study, however. The entry frequency matrix is designed primarily to address a second issue: the effect of corporate experience on location decisions. Before we get to that issue, it has to be remembered that Table 2-4 is based on SIC 3-digit observations. This table reflects only the parent's first manufacturing decisions in each country for a given industry. The international spread of manufacturing for subsequent products is not captured in this table. In order to analyze trends in the manufacturing sequence over time more effectively, we turn now to a body of data based on individual products.

Table 2-5 represents a similar set of entry frequencies based on analysis of 954 individual new products. Note that there are few significant changes in the order of priority and the magnitude of entry frequencies in comparison with Table 2-4. The United Kingdom exhibits entry frequencies slightly higher than Canada in this table, and Australia follows these two nations in terms of priority. Japan exhibits a significantly higher priority in Table 2-5, although West Germany appears much lower in the sequence for these products on the average. The only other nation to move more than two places in the sequence is Spain, falling from ninth place in Table 2-4 to thirteenth in Table 2-5.

One reason for the differences between these two tables may lie in the chronological distributions of the two samples. The individual products data are relatively more recent. Further examination of the effects of time may shed light on reasons for stability or change in manufacturing sequences.

In order to examine trends over time, the data in Table 2-5 were divided into three subsets. Products were classified according to whether they were first introduced in the U.S. between 1945-54, 1955-64, or 1965-75. A table similar to Table 2-5 was compiled for each of these three subsets. These tables appear in Appendix IV.

Analysis of these tables reveals some slight but significant changes in the

TABLE 2-5

Frequency by which Investment for 954 Individual Products Occurred in Country A before Country B, 1945-1978

Country B

Country A	1	2	3	4	5	6	7	8	9	10	11	12	13	14	15	16	17	18	19	20	Total
1. UK		.500	.635	.678	.683	.720	.731	.722	.771	.803	.879	.839	.867	.902	.924	.941	.934	.977	.983	.991	15.480
2. Canada			.609	.656	.654	.716	.692	.705	.756	.779	.850	.866	.866	.907	.909	.939	.947	.982	.982	.988	15.303
3. Australia				.542	.561	.602	.622	.606	.670	.707	.793	.775	.805	.862	.892	.925	.910	.963	.978	.989	13.958
4. France					.503	.550	.556	.552	.648	.683	.772	.733	.781	.820	.858	.903	.898	.965	.973	.987	13.306
5. Japan						.541	.556	.546	.633	.715	.735	.745	.772	.791	.831	.895	.902.	.963	.975	.983	13.192
6. W. Germany							.509	.505	.583	.629	.683	.705	.704	.777	.806	.844	.879	.943	.968	.984	12.590
7. Mexico								.503	.569	.632	.728	.702	.748	.798	.828	.884	.891	.954	.972	.986	12.529
8. Mexico									.596	.641	.726	.707	.768	.781	.851	.890	.894	.961	.971	.990	11.837
9. Italy										.554	.633	.625	.665	.695	.776	.854	.834	.942	.961	.974	11.362
10. Belgium											.553	.569	.577	.624	.680	.773	.786	.913	.951	.975	10.258
11. Colombia												.503	.560	.572	.684	.758	.762	.894	.953	.971	9.598
12. Netherlands													.515	.553	.632	.733	.744	.906	.935	.967	9.216
13. Spain														.529	.604	.707	.748	.901	.938	.968	8.767
14. S. Africa															.566	.676	.728	.874	.926	.962	8.255
15. Argentina																.632	.677	.857	.923	.952	7.190
16. India																	.529	.727	.745	.900	5.677
17. Philippines																			.838	.889	4.959
18. S. Korea																			.647	.750	3.148
19. Taiwan																				.600	2.131
20. Ireland																					1.194
																					190.00

manufacturing sequence over time. Japan moves from eighth to fourth in the sequence, while Brazil, Mexico, Colombia, India, and South Africa decline more than two places between the first and third periods. Italy, the Netherlands, Belgium, and Taiwan each move up the list more than two places between 1945-54 and 1965-75. The position of Canada, the U.K., and Australia in the manufacturing sequence do not change throughout the period.

This pattern lends an impression of stability in location patterns. However, values for some country entry frequencies have changed significantly over time. This trend can be seen by examining values in rows for Canada, the United Kingdom, and Australia in each of the three matrices from Appendix IV. Examination of these data in Table 2-6 shows a distinct shift in emphasis from Canada to other nations. Eighteen of the nineteen entry frequencies for Canada are lower for products introduced between 1955-64 than for products introduced in the 1945-54 period. In addition, 13 of the 19 frequencies are lower in the third period than in the second. Although Canada's position in the manufacturing sequence has not changed, there has been a subtle but distinct reduction in preference for Canada as a manufacturing site relative to other countries. Similar, although less significant, trends have affected the United Kingdom and Australia.

Examination of foreign manufacturing sequences for these three time periods suggests that changes in locational emphasis have occurred. In addition to a number of changes in positions in the sequences over time, a more subtle shift has affected countries such as the United Kingdom, Canada, and Australia. What factors contributed to this shift?

The basic effects of market size, political climate, and financial factors can again be applied to this question. Market growth can be associated with the improved positions of Japan and Italy. An increase in political risk and the imposition of stringent financial and ownership controls can be related to India's decline, while increased political risk may also be related to the slide in South Africa's position. However, a more pervasive force than relative changes in market size or political risk may be at work here.

The powerful influence that market similarity appears to exert on location patterns suggests another effect. Why does similarity encourage manufacturing? Similarity results in increased demand and supply for a product. On the demand side, consumers in similar markets adopt products designed in response to needs which approximate their own more quickly than consumers in other markets. On the supply side, the high transferability of marketing, technology, and human resources stimulates manufacturing activity in similar markets. Market similarity also reduces management uncertainty levels. Consumer response to a new product is always unpredictable, but the possibility of an unanticipated negative response can be minimized by first introducing it in markets which are most similar to the

TABLE 2-6

Entry Frequencies for Canada, the U.K. and
Australia, by Time Period

Period of U.S. Introduction for Product	Country B																			
	1	2	3	4	5	6	7	8	9	10	11	12	13	14	15	16	17	18	19	20
Canada																				
1945-54	.550	-	.653	.783	.750	.667	.803	.828	.902	.862	.859	.932	.905	.934	.905	.950	.983	.999	.999	.999
1955-64	.478	-	.627	.663	.639	.749	.653	.749	.757	.777	.827	.860	.833	.923	.903	.906	.973	.993	.983	.993
1965-75	.507	-	.574	.599	.638	.645	.730	.640	.699	.748	.876	.846	.891	.574	.917	.976	.903	.976	.976	.961
U. Kingdom																				
1945-54	-	.450	.614	.697	.803	.825	.708	.768	.852	.839	.852	.898	.900	.864	.933	.931	1.00	1.00	1.00	1.00
1955-64	-	.522	.698	.710	.708	.767	.788	.700	.803	.855	.886	.824	.861	.916	.917	.916	.949	.971	.994	.994
1965-75	-	.493	.571	.632	.612	.629	.673	.734	.702	.732	.881	.835	.860	.899	.929	.983	.903	.975	.959	.983
Australia																				
1945-54	.386	.347	-	.603	.717	.655	.606	.656	.774	.800	.737	.860	.821	.852	.923	.904	.980	1.00	1.00	1.00
1955-64	.302	.373	-	.528	.500	.623	.671	.541	.654	.697	.769	.717	.771	.876	.876	.891	.921	.943	.993	.991
1965-74	.429	.424	-	.575	.539	.558	.580	.672	.651	.681	.851	.810	.839	.851	.851	.980	.868	.970	.952	.980

home market. Consumer response and returns in such markets will closely approximate those in the home market. These forces lead firms to prefer investment in countries such as Canada, the United Kingdom, and Australia over other nations.

As firms gain operating experience in additional markets, however, the effect of uncertainty declines. When scale economies, learning benefits, and uncertainty reduction can be realized in additional nations, projects in those countries will become relatively more attractive and market preferences will change. As these experience effects accumulate in many countries, the attraction of similar markets will decline.

Firms with extensive foreign experience in many markets will exhibit less locational preference for markets similar to their home country.[16] However, this process occurs gradually as experience is accumulated. The gradual decline in emphasis for the United Kingdom, Canada, and Australia suggests the evolutionary nature of this process. This process may also explain the decline of Mexico, Brazil, and Colombia in the manufacturing sequence. The geographic proximity of these nations and the long tradition of U.S. activity in Latin America suggest that these nations might be perceived as near and familiar despite many dissimilarities.

The accumulation of information and scale economies places distant, dissimilar markets on a more equal basis in comparison with near and familiar markets. It can be hypothesized that the position of more distant and unfamiliar markets in the manufacturing sequence will improve as firms gain experience in such nations.

A general test of this hypothesis can be conducted by using the frequency matrix to test the effects of experience on location and sequence decisions. Specifically, the presence or absence of an existing manufacturing facility in an individual country can be hypothesized to have an effect on that country's position in the manufacturing sequence for products of a given firm.

To test this hypothesis, four conditional entry frequency matrices were compiled. Each of these matrices tabulates country-pair manufacturing priorities under a specific condition. The four such conditions are:

1. NN—The firm was not present in either country at the time manufacturing was initiated in one of the two countries.

2. PN—The firm was present in the first country, but not in the second country at the time manufacturing was initiated in the first country.

3. NP—The firm was not present in the first country and present in the second country at the time manufacturing was initiated in the first country.

4.   PP—The firm was present in both countries when manufacturing was initiated in one of the countries.

The tables derived from this exercise appear in Appendix V.[17]

The conditional entry frequencies in these tables can be compared to determine how the presence of an existing manufacturing facility in a country affects its position in the manufacturing sequence. A test can be conducted by subtracting one matrix from another. If firms exhibit a greater preference for a country when it has existing facilities, the PN rates for any country-pair should be higher than the NN, PP or NP rates.

Algebraically, the hypothesis can be stated as:

$$F_{ij_{PN}} \geq F_{ij_{NN}}, \quad F_{ij_{PP}}, \quad F_{ij_{NP}}.$$

This test involves subtracting each cell in one matrix from its counterpart in a second matrix.

The results of this exercise appear below. The PN entry frequencies are consistently higher than entry frequencies exhibited when the firm is present in neither country, or when it is present in both countries. The most significant comparison, as might be expected, is with the NP frequencies; the rates at which firms produce first in one country of a pair when they are not present in that first country but present in the second. For example, entry frequencies for the same country-pair are higher in the PN table than in the NP table for 312 out of 348 cases. These differences in conditional entry frequencies support the proposition that the presence of an existing manufacturing subsidiary in a country stimulates the parent to initiate manufacturing in that nation.

Figure 2-2
A Test of the Effects of Prior Presence in a Host Country on Location
Priorities: Comparison of Conditional Country-Pair Entry Frequencies

Matrices Subtracted	Positive Observations	Negative Observations	Sign-test Coefficient	Probability of Significance
PN-NN	276	72	4.08	.01
PN-PP	282	66	4.37	.01
PN-NP	312	36	5.49	.01

This test effectively eliminates any intervening effects due to market size, political climate, geographic proximity, or market similarity in testing the effects of experience on location patterns. While absolute entry frequency rates reflect the effects of these other factors, this test measures how the presence or absence of existing facilities leads to variations in individual frequencies, regardless of any other characteristics of the nation. The results suggest that this factor significantly influences location decisions.

At this point in the analysis, three broad trends have been identified. First, manufacturing activity is highly correlated with market size, which appears to serve as a proxy for the effects of production economics and oligopoly factors on foreign manufacturing decisions. Second, firms exhibit a significant preference for manufacturing in similar markets. Third, the presence of existing manufacturing facilities exerts a significant positive effect on foreign manufacturing decisions.

These findings, combined with the observation that entry frequencies for Canada, the United Kingdom, and Australia are declining over time, suggests that the position of more unfamiliar markets in the manufacturing sequence will improve as firms gain experience in such nations. Conditional entry frequences can again be utilized to examine this hypothesis. Priorities exhibited when the firm is present in both nations of a country-pair can be compared to those seen when the firm is not present in either country. The PP and NN tables in Appendix V serve this purpose.

A comparison of these two tables reveals several major shifts in position in the sequence. Japan appears in the tenth position when the firm is not present in either nation of a country-pair. When the firm is present in both nations, Japan ranks fourth in priority. Mexico, Brazil, and Colombia's position in the sequence declines substantially when the firm is present. The other nations remain generally in equivalent positions under these two conditions. The positions of Canada, the United Kingdom, and Australia do not change at all.

This pattern seems not to support the hypothesis that the attraction of similar markets will decline as firms gain experience in other nations. However, there is again a major difference between entry frequencies in these two tables. Analysis of aggregate entry frequencies reveals sharp variances between the two matrices. As seen in Figure 2-3, the aggregate measures of priority for Canada, the United Kingdom, Australia, Mexico, Brazil, Colombia, and Argentina all show substantial declines between the NN matrix and the PP matrix. Even more striking, however, is the fact that the cumulative entry frequencies of West Germany and France are also lower when the firm already manufactures at rival locations.

These shifts in priority may to some extent reflect shifts in market size or political climate, as the observations in the matrix are more recent. Such effects cannot explain why the cumulative frequency for India is higher in the PP matrix, however. These factors also cannot explain the reduction in cumulative frequencies for Brazil, West Germany, and France. Something more significant is at work here.

Figure 2-3

A Comparison of Location Priorities Under Conditions
of Presence or No Prior Presence in Host Countries:
Aggregate Entry Frequencies for Twenty Host Countries

Nation	Sum of Entry Frequencies from Country Row in NN Matrix	Sum of Entry Frequencies from Country Row in PP Matrix	Difference
Canada	17.471	13.743	-3.728
U. Kingdom	15.581	13.386	-2.195
Mexico	14.000	11.566	-2.434
W. Germany	13.047	12.043	-1.004
Brazil	13.007	10.766	-2.241
France	12.753	11.569	-1.184
Australia	12.253	11.279	- .974
Colombia	10.975	9.638	-1.337
Spain	10.091	10.306	.215
Japan	10.056	11.614	1.558
Italy	9.845	9.909	.064
Argentina	8.778	7.573	-1.205
S. Africa	8.584	7.881	- .703
Belgium	8.412	10.030	1.618
Netherlands	7.795	10.328	2.533
India	7.391	7.761	.370
Philippines	3.582	4.158	.576
Ireland	3.144	6.524	3.380
Taiwan	1.622	6.206	4.584
S. Korea	1.613	3.720	2.107
	190.00	190.00	0

NOTE: Aggregate Entry Frequency for country i $= \sum_{j=1}^{20} FC_{ij}$

The NN matrix tabulates entry frequencies when the parent has no
prior manufacturing presence in either country being compared.

The PP matrix tabulates entry frequencies when the parent is
already present in both countries being compared.

The changes in cumulative frequencies show a consistent pattern. The high priority nations generally have lost their wide edge over secondary markets as preferred manufacturing sites. The first eight nations in the NN sequence all show significantly lower cumulative frequencies in the PP matrix. Ten of the twelve secondary nations in the NN list show increased cumulative frequencies in the second matrix.

This trend suggests a broader process is at work. Firms established in many markets do not discount secondary markets as much as firms not yet active in those markets. Once facilities are initially established in secondary markets, the uncertainty premium initially associated with such markets falls quickly. The process of incremental international expansion shows itself strongly in these data.

The effect of experience on location patterns is twofold. Firms prefer nations in which they operate existing facilities over those in which they do not, ceteris paribus. In addition, firms with established manufacturing networks exhibit less preference for the near, similar, and more familiar markets over markets that others may perceive as less attractive because of high uncertainty levels.

Experience also affects other aspects of foreign manufacturing activity. Sequence reflects location preferences, but it also reflects timing decisions. Timing is a second key variable in the international spread of U.S. manufacturing.

Timing Patterns

The effect of experience on location raises an important issue. If the presence of foreign subsidiaries influences location patterns, do the existence and expansion of foreign subsidiary networks lead to more rapid and extensive spread of manufacturing for U.S. products abroad? This section deals only with the spread of manufacturing to affiliates in which the U.S. parent owns 5 percent or more of the firm's equity. Transfers to independent licensees will be addressed in the next section.

In order to address this and other issues, three variables were defined to capture distinct aspects of timing patterns. The first variable, *initial transfer lag*, measures the number of years between the introduction of a product in the United States and its first production in a foreign subsidiary of the introducing firm. The term transfer is used to signify the initiation of foreign manufacturing for a product. This second variable, *transfer rate*, measures the average number of foreign subsidiaries initiating manufacture of the product in each year following the first such case. The third variable, *transfer ratio*, reflects the percentage of products in any given subset that have been produced abroad in at least one foreign subsidiary by the end of 1977. These variables are designed to address the basic questions: Was the product manufactured abroad? When was it first manufactured abroad? At what rate did manufacturing spread abroad? These three variables will serve to measure trends in timing patterns for the sample of 954 new products which provide the basis for this analysis. Examination of this sample reveals several distinct trends in foreign manufacturing activity for products developed in the U.S.

Products introduced in recent years have tended to appear abroad much more quickly than those introduced early in the postwar period. Initial transfer lags, in particular, have shortened dramatically. As Table 2-7 indicates, less than 10 percent of all 174 products introduced in the U.S. between 1945-49 were produced abroad within one year. By comparison, over 32 percent of the products introduced between 1970-75 had been produced abroad within one year of their U.S. introduction. New products are being manufactured abroad much more quickly than in the past.

There is also a significant trend in average annual transfer rates. Products introduced between 1945-49 in the U.S. spread abroad at the rate of .212 transfers per year in the years after their first foreign facility was established. The annual rate increases steadily for more recent innovations, peaking at .718 transfers per year for the 1970-75 subset.

Part of this variation in transfer rates is simply a result of the product's age. Transfer activity tends to follow a typical S-shaped growth curve, so that transfer rates decline after the years of peak activity. Consequently, transfer rates for older products will be lower, ceteris paribus, than for more recent products. To remove this effect, a second transfer rate was calculated which measures the average annual number of transfers in the three years immediately following the first such transfer. As can be seen in Table 2-7, there is significantly less variance in this measure, although a steady increase in transfer rate sill occurs over time.

A number of hypotheses can be developed to explain the trends toward more rapid and extensive transfer activity. Although any time-correlated variable will correlate highly with these transfer timing patterns, the true test of any hypothesis will be cross-sectional analysis. Among those tested in this study, measures of the firm's experience emerge as generally and consistently significant in explaining transfer timing patterns.

The Experience Factor and Timing Decisions

This section will examine the premise that the application of scale economies, learning benefits and reduced certainty to transfer decisions results in more rapid and extensive spread of manufacturing abroad. These effects raise the returns on foreign investment projects and stimulate the spread of manufacturing abroad. Let us first examine the correlation between the firm's general international experience and timing patterns.

Although many measures of general international experience can be

TABLE 2-7

Initial Transfer Lag, Transfer Ratio and Average Transfer Rate
for 954 Products: By Period of U.S. Introduction

Period of U.S. Introduction	Number of Products	Initial Transfer Lag % First Introduced Abroad in:					Transfer Ratio % Introduced abroad as of 12/77	Average Annual Transfer Rate from Year of First Foreign Production to:	
		One year or less	Two to three years	Four to five years	Six to nine years	Ten or more years		Three years thereafter	1977 year-end
1945 - 49	174	8.0%	9.2%	8.0%	16.7%	46.6%	88.5%	.843	.212
1950 - 54	151	8.6	9.3	12.6	25.8	28.4	84.1	.919	.236
1955 - 59	153	8.5	15.7	17.6	23.6	19.6	85.0	.901	.205
1960 - 64	185	23.2	19.4	14.6	13.5	9.9	80.6	.941	.314
1965 - 69	170	28.2	16.5	11.8	7.1	(a)	63.6	1.018	.433
1970 - 75	121	32.2	18.1	(a)	(a)	(a)	50.3	1.311	.718
Total	954	17.7%	14.1%	11.7%	14.7%	18.1%	76.3%	.952	.308

Note: Average annual transfer rates are compiled for individual products by dividing the number of transfers in a period by the total number of years since the first case of foreign manufacturing for the product. These individual rates are then averaged to yield annual rates for subsets of the data base. In compiling this average rate, products which have not been manufactured abroad are excluded.

(s): Not applicable.

developed, one measure applies specifically to international manufacturing activity. This measure, labeled "number of prior transfers," tabulates the number of times a firm has initiated manufacturing for new products in its foreign subsidiaries. The cumulative number of such transfers represents a measure of the firm's general experience in initiating manufacturing in foreign subsidiaries.

Transfer timing patterns were analyzed with respect to the firm's number of prior transfers at the time of U.S. introduction for each product. As can be seen in Table 2-8, significant variations in transfer timing exist. Products introduced by firms with the least prior transfer activity spread abroad at much slower rates than products introduced by parents with more prior transfer experience. The percentage of products produced abroad within one year increases from 10.2 percent for firms with less than 10 transfers to 27.0 percent for firms with more than 30 transfers. Aggregate transfer rates increase from .224 to .429 per year.

There are substantial risks in interpreting the results of a simple cross-tabulation of this sort. These results are particularly susceptible to intervening effects, as the number of prior transfers is closely correlated with time. The correlation matrix in Appendix I reveals a correlation coefficient of .698 for number of prior transfers and the year of U.S. introduction for a product. The effects of this relationship can be seen in transfer ratios. While 82.6 percent of the products introduced by firms with fewer than 10 transfers have been produced abroad, only 70.0 percent of the products in the more than 30 transfers group had been produced abroad by the end of 1977. Transfer ratios are lower for more recent products, as seen distinctly in Table 2-7. However, when the time factor is held constant in later cross-sectional analyses, initial lag and transfer rate trends remain significantly higher for firms with extensive experience, and the transfer ratio pattern reverses. Despite the risks that cross-tabulations can lead to faulty conclusions, they will be used here to provide a more detailed view of transfer timing patterns. All the relationships shown are supported by further multivariate analysis.

It should be noted that the categories in Table 2-8 do not represent distinct sets of U.S. firms. A single firm will appear in each of the categories in this and other tables. The objective of this analysis is to identify characteristics of the firm at the time a product is introduced in the U.S. and to relate these characteristics to timing patterns.

General experience appears to stimulate foreign manufacturing activity. It is also important to consider specific experience variables. As seen in the analysis of manufacturing sequences, experience in specific countries has an important influence on foreign manufacturing activity.

TABLE 2-8

Initial Transfer Lag, Transfer Ratio and Average Transfer Rate
for 954 Products: By Parent's Aggregate Number of
Prior Transfers at Time of U.S. Introduction

Parent's Aggregate Number of Prior Transfers	Number of Products	Initial Transfer Lag % First Introduced Abroad in:					Transfer Ratio % Introduced abroad as of 12/77	Average Annual Transfer Rate from Year of First Foreign Production to:	
		One year or less	Two to three years	Four to five years	Six to nine years	Ten or more years		Three years thereafter	1977 year-end
0 - 10	334	10.2%	11.4%	11.4%	13.8%	35.9%	82.6%	.597	.224
11 - 29	254	14.5	15.3	10.2	21.2	16.1	77.3	.811	.268
30 or more	366	27.0	15.6	13.1	10.9	3.3	70.0	1.305	.429
Total	954	17.7%	14.1%	11.7%	14.7%	18.1%	76.3%	.952	.308

Note: Prior transfers are compiled by adding all cases of initiation of manufacturing for SIC 3-digit industries at any foreign location before 1945, plus all cases of transfer for individual new products thereafter.

Specific Experience

An important specific experience variable is the firm's prior activity in individual countries. If experience has an effect on manufacturing decisions, firms will prefer countries in which they have extensive prior experience as manufacturing sites. Prior activity implies that economies of scale can be realized on existing manufacturing facilities and other resources, and that the firm's level of uncertainty will be reduced. The learning benefits of prior activity in the country provide additional stimulus to initiate manufacturing.

In order to examine the effect of experience in specific countries on timing patterns, the time lag between introduction of a new product in the U.S. and commencement of manufacturing in individual foreign nations was measured. This lag was then compared to the firm's number of prior transfers into that host country at the time manufacturing was initiated.

An aggregate tabulation based on this approach appears in Table 2-9. A clear trend can be observed in this table. Of the transfers to nations in which the parent had completed 10 or more prior transfers, 24.6 percent were within one year of the product's U.S. introduction. Of the 433 transfers to nations in which the parent had no prior manufacturing experience, only 5.5 percent occurred within one year of the product's U.S. introduction.

Although these results suggest that prior experience in a particular country encourages more rapid transfer, they are highly subject to the effects of intervening variables. Number of prior transfers is correlated with time, market size, proximity, and market similarity, for example. However, when individual recipient nations are examined to permit cross-sectional analysis of the effect of prior transfer experience on introduction lag, the trend shown earlier is confirmed. Firms tend to introduce products more rapidly into any given nation when they have extensive prior experience in that nation.

Another dimension of experience also should be considered. The firm's level of transfer activity also varies by industry, and this may affect foreign manufacturing patterns for products in different industries. To measure industry experience, prior transfers were calculated for individual SIC 3-digit industries. Because firms have entered new industries over time, this variable is far less susceptible to intervening effects than the aggregate transfer variable.

As Table 2-10 indicates, there is a clear trend toward more rapid transfer when the firm has extensive foreign manufacturing experience in the product's industry. Where 13.3 percent of the products introduced by parents with less than three prior transfers in the product's industry appear abroad within one year, 23.0 percent of the products introduced by parents with more than 10 prior transfers were manufactured abroad within one year. A similar trend exists for transfer rate, and the transfer ratio increases as prior transfer experience increases as well.

TABLE 2-9

Transfer Lags for 3,357 Transfers of 954
Products: Classified by Parent's Number of Prior Transfers to Host
Country at Time of Transfer

Transfers Classified by Numbers of Prior Transfers of Parent to Host Country	Number of Transfers of 954 Products	Transfers to Foreign Subsidiaries, by Number of Years Following U.S. Introduction				
		One Year or Less After	Two to Three Years After	Four to Five Years After	Six to Nine Years After	Ten or More Years After
0	433	5.5%	13.4%	11.5%	17.3%	52.2%
1 - 4	1,226	8.2	13.5	11.2	17.2	49.8
5 - 9	746	15.8	10.6	10.0	21.2	42.5
10 or More	500	24.6	13.2	8.4	19.8	34.0
Unknown	451	11.7	8.0	2.4	14.4	53.4
Total	3,357	12.5%	12.1%	10.7%	18.1%	46.6%

Note: Transfer lag equals the number of years between introduction of an innovation in the U.S. and production in a host country.

TABLE 2-10

Initial Transfer Lag, Transfer Ratio and Average Transfer Rate for 954 Products: By Parent's Number of Prior Transfers in Product's Industry at Time of U.S. Introduction

Parent's Number of Prior Transfers in Product's Industry	Number of Products	Initial Transfer Lag % First Introduced Abroad in:					Transfer Ratio % Introduced abroad as of 12/77	Average Annual Transfer Rate from Year of First Foreign Production to:	
		One year or less	Two to three years	Four to five years	Six to nine years	Ten or more years		Three years thereafter	1977 year-end
0 - 2	470	13.3%	12.5%	11.2%	15.3%	18.1%	70.5%	.821	.238
3 - 10	175	20.5	19.4	13.1	12.6	15.4	81.1	.963	.306
11 or more	309	23.0	13.3	11.7	14.9	19.7	82.5	1.114	.401
Total	954	17.7%	14.1%	11.7%	14.7%	18.1%	76.3%	.952	.308

Prior transfers are measured above at the level of SIC 3-digit industries. Prior transfers can also be measured for individual products. Teece has noted that the cost of initiating manufacturing at new sites declines as the number of prior transfers for a product increases.[18] If so, transfer experience will lead to more rapid subsequent transfer activity for a product. One simple means of testing this hypothesis involves examination of the time interval between individual cases of transfer for a product. The effects of experience could contribute to a decreasing time interval between instances of transfer for individual products.

Time intervals between cases of transfer were compiled for each of the 728 products that have been produced abroad by 1977. Intervals were computed by measuring the number of years that had elapsed since the last preceding transfer. These intervals can then be aggregated to yield the average time lapse between successive cases of transfer.

After the first foreign introduction, an average of 3.3 years passed before a second transfer was initiated. The time interval between the second and third transfer averages 2.4 years. This interval steadily declines as the number of transfers increases, supporting the proposition that specific product-related transfer experience stimulates foreign manufacturing activity.

Figure 2-4
Average Number of Years between Successive
Transfers for 728 Products

Transfer Sequence	Years from Last Previous Transfer (Average)
First	—
Second	3.3
Third	2.4
Fourth	2.3
Fifth	2.1
Sixth	1.7
Seventh	1.6
Eighth	1.3
Ninth	1.4
Tenth	1.4

Each of the measures of general and specific experience correlates highly with transfer timing patterns. They appear to be closely related to the speed, rate, and extent of foreign manufacturing activity. However, analysis of these variables is hampered by several problems. First, there is the significant correlation between time and the measures of transfer timing used as dependent variables in this analysis. More recent innovations exhibit shorter initial transfer lags, faster transfer rates, and lower transfer ratios. As a result of this correlation, there is a strong possibility that statistical tests will be subject to intervening effects associated with time. For example, any time-correlated independent variable will correlate highly with the dependent measures of transfer activity. The measures of experience are in fact highly time-correlated. Aggregate transfers and year of U.S. introduction show a correlation coefficient of .698; transfers in specific industries show a coefficient of .427 with year of U.S. introduction.

In addition to the possibility of intervening effects, problems associated with collinearity among the independent variables may also arise. Examination of the correlation matrix in Appendix I reveals that a number of simple correlation coefficients among independent variables are .50 or more.

The possibility of interaction effects among the independent variables must also be considered. There are intuitive reasons to question the assumption of additivity in multivariate analyses of this sample.

Several approaches were used to address the problems of intervening effects, collinearity, and interactions among the independent variables. To minimize the possibility that time-series analysis could present misleading statistical relationships, cross-sectional analysis was used to further examine individual independent variables. This approach also served to minimize the effects of collinearity. The extent and effects of interactions among independent variables are examined primarily through F-tests derived from analysis of variance. If one independent variable proved to be distributed closely with another, dummy variables were used to isolate possible interactions between independent variables in further analyses.

Multivariate tests were conducted for the entire 1945-77 period. Cross-sectional analyses were then conducted to test the time-adjusted relationship between these variables and transfer timing patterns. The results of these tests appear in Appendix III.

The relationship between experience and foreign manufacturing activity is strongly supported by these tests. Significant correlations between measures of experience and transfer timing variables exist in both time-series and cross-section analyses. These tests support the proposition that increased experience stimulates the initiation of manufacturing for U.S. products in foreign subsidiaries.

Direct Investment and Licensing

If increased experience stimulates manufacturing of U.S. products in foreign subsidiaries, what effect will experience have on the choice between direct investment and licensing in inititating foreign manufacturing? If the economics of direct investment are enhanced by experience effects, the firms' valuation of foreign investment projects relative to licensing arrangements will increase. With everything else equal, increased experience will influence the firms' decisions in favor of direct investment.

Individual product data can be used to test the relationship between experience and patterns of direct investment and licensing. Licensing activity is defined as the contracted manufacture of a product by an independent foreign firm with no significant equity ties to the U.S. firm. A slightly smaller sample will be used for this purpose. Of the 57 firms in this study, only 32 cooperated in providing full data on licensing activity. This analysis is based on these 32 firms and the 580 products they have introduced in the U.S. since 1945.

Of the 580 products in this subset, 434 have been manufactured in at least one foreign country. By the end of 1977, manufacturing for these 434 products had been initiated at 1,843 foreign locations. Over one-quarter of these observations were initiated by independent licensees of the U.S. firm. An additional 17.1 percent were initiated by companies in which the U.S. firm had a minority equity interest. Together, over 40.0 percent of all transfers were to independent licensees and minority-owned affiliates.

This ratio may exceed initial expectations, especially when it is noted that the data is drawn from a sample of 32 large, established multinational enterprises. Part of the answer is that the heaviest use of licensing occurred in the early postwar period. The rate of licensing relative to direct investment has declined over time. For products introduced in the U.S. during the 1946-55 period, independent licensees and minority-owned affiliates initiated 47.4 percent of all cases of foreign manufacturing. For products introduced in the 1966-75 period, such parties account for only 22.8 percent of all transfers.

There is no a priori reason to expect this relative decline in licensing activity. On the contrary, a number of trends in the environment support the opposite contention. Many nations have adopted restrictions on direct investment to stimulate transfer of technology via licensing.[19] This trend is increasingly important in the less-developed world, and represents a key issue in the North-South debate. Host countries are becoming increasingly capable of acquiring technology via licenses as the number of global competitors in many industries has grown substantially.[20] This permits host countries to negotiate more effectively with alternative suppliers of any given technology and gain more favorable terms. This trend suggests an increase in licensing activity.

In the industrialized world, the growth of competitors may also encourage licensing activity. The presence of large established local firms in a foreign market may deter direct investment by U.S. firms. The classic cross-licensing arrangements between ICI and DuPont arose from such a situation, for example.[21] The presence of such firms abroad also provides a more efficient external market for technology. These firms will place a higher value on licensing arrangements because of their own concern for stability, their perception of mutual benefits from two-way flows of technology, lower technical uncertainty, and the value placed on an ongoing relationship with the licensor. The continuing growth of foreign competition may thus encourage licensing in the industrial nations. Why then do the data reveal a decline in licensing activity?

The reduction in the use of licensing can be related to the underlying expansion of foreign subsidiary networks. The choice between direct investment and licensing becomes much simpler, if not a foregone conclusion, when the firm has a subsidiary in the market in question. The presence of a subsidiary in a market generally dictates the use of direct investment when foreign manufacturing is warranted in that market.

Table 2-11
Transfers of 580 Products: Classified by Type of
Recipient and Period of U.S. Introduction

Percentage of Transfers to:

Period of U.S. Intro- duction	Inde- pendent Licensees	Minority- owned Joint Ventures	Majority- owned Joint Ventures	Wholly- owned Subsidiaries	Total Number
1946-55	29.2%	18.2%	6.2%	46.3%	982
1956-65	23.6	20.1	4.5	51.9	628
1966-75	18.1	4.7	3.9	73.4	233
TOTAL	25.9%	17.1%	5.3%	51.6%	1,843

Note: Minority-owned joint ventures are those owned 50% or less by the U.S. parent.

The investment or licensing decision in such cases will be strongly biased toward direct investment for several reasons. Scale economies in the use of human resources as well as marketing and manufacturing resources will enhance the economics of direct investment. The firm's uncertainty about profit streams to be derived from the project will also be reduced because of greater knowledge of local conditions.

The existence of a prior licensing agreement in the country in question can also affect this decision. The U.S. firm might prefer to license if it has an existing relationship with an independent firm in the market. Such a pattern, characteristic of cross-licensing agreements, is also common in certain types of direct licensing contracts. Many licensing agreements specify that the licensee shall receive rights to all current and future technology of the licensor within a specified industry. In such cases, the U.S. licensor would be legally barred from direct investment.

However, while the presence of a subsidiary generally overrules the use of licensing, the presence of a licensee does not preclude direct investment. Many firms use licensing as a low-risk means of initially testing markets for their products. As the firm's experience and confidence increases, its willingness to make a greater commitment may lead it to form a joint venture or a wholly-owned subsidiary.

The data in Table 2-12 reveal several trends that support these general statements. Approximately 59.5 percent of all transfers to nations in which the firm had an existing licensing agreement were conducted via licensing agreements. For transfers to nations in which the firm had no prior direct investment or licensing activity, 31.8 percent were conducted via license.

For nations in which the firm had at least one prior transfer to a subsidiary, licensing activity drops off sharply and continues to fall as the number of transfers increases. Once the firm has made a direct investment in a country, subsidiaries account for over 80.0 percent of all further transfers.

The fact that independent licensing activity continues after establishment of a subsidiary may surprise some observers. Such activity generally occurs in lines unrelated to those of the existing subsidiary. Also, it generally occurs in situations where the firm holds only a minority interest in an existing subsidiary. It is quite common in Japan, for example, for a U.S. firm to hold a minority interest in a joint venture manufacturing one product while negotiating a license with an independent firm for another line.

Industry Experience

The parent's status and prior experience in any country have a significant effect on recipient decisions for that country. The firm's prior experience in a product's industry also appears to influence these decisions. For products in industries in which the firm had no prior transfer experience, licensing accounts for 32.0 percent of all transfers. As the firm's number of transfers increases, the rate of licensing drops significantly. Licensing accounts for only 10.9 percent of all transfers for products in industries in which the parent has more than 10 prior transfers.

The relationships between country and industry experience and type of recipient patterns are quite strong in the simple cross-tabulations presented here. However, these relationships are again subject to problems of intervening effects and collinearity. These relationships must be examined under statistical tests that control for these effects. In developing these tests, it

TABLE 2-12

Transfers of 580 Products: Classified by Type of Recipient and
Parent's Status in Host Country at Time of Transfer

Transfers Classi- fied by Parent's Status in Host Country at Time of Transfer	Percentage of Transfers Via:				Total Number
	Independent Licensees	Minority- owned Affiliates	Majority- owned Affiliates	Wholly- owned Affiliates	
No Prior Transfer Activity	31.8%	17.5%	7.2%	44.5%	236
Prior Licensing Agreement Only	59.5	7.4	5.4	27.6	257
Prior Direct Investments	17.2	18.4	4.8	59.6	1,350
Number of Trans- fers					
1 to 2	20.4	20.7	6.6	52.3	396
3 to 10	16.0	17.9	4.7	61.4	725
11 or more	15.3	16.1	2.2	66.4	229
Total	25.9%	17.1%	5.2%	51.6%	1,843

is important to note that recipient patterns are strongly influenced by characteristics of the host country in question. Table 2-14 presents recipient patterns for transfers to a number of different nations. The relative use of licensing, joint-ventures, and wholly-owned subsidiaries varies widely.

Licensing accounts for 45.9 percent of all transfers to Japan, but only 5.0 percent, of transfers to Canada. Other nations which exhibit relatively high rates of licensing include Peru, Venezuela, Netherlands, West Germany, Sweden, Switzerland, South Africa, India, and Turkey. On the other hand, Colombia, Australia, Mexico, Brazil, Argentina, and the United Kingdom exhibit relatively low rates of licensing activity. What factors result in high or low rates of licensing activity?

It is notable that the countries with the lowest rates of licensing are those that appeared high in the manufacturing sequence in the first section of this chapter. The near and familiar countries—Canada, the United Kingdom, Australia, Colombia, Mexico, and Brazil all exhibit significantly lower than average rates of licensing. This pattern in itself suggests that experience factors strongly influence investment and licensing decisions. In nations where scale economies can readily be realized and where uncertainty is low, direct investment is preferred over licensing. This suggests that licensing will

Table 2-13
Transfers of 580 Products, Classified by Type of Recipient and Prior Transfers in Product's Industry at Time of U.S. Introduction

Transfers Classified by Parent's Number of Prior Transfers in Product's Industry	Percentage of Transfers Via:				
	Independent Licensees	Minority-owned Affiliates*	Majority-owned Affiliates	Wholly-owned Affiliates	Total Number
0 Prior Transfers	32.0%	17.1%	3.7%	47.2%	870
1-4 Prior Transfers	24.3	15.6	6.9	53.2	518
5-10 Prior Transfers	22.4	18.9	4.6	54.1	216
11 or More Transfers	10.9	13.0	7.1	69.0	239
TOTAL	25.9%	17.1%	5.3%	51.6%	1,843

* Minority-owned affiliates include companies owned 50% or less by a U.S. parent.

TABLE 2-14

Transfers of 580 Products, Classified by Type of
Recipient and Host Country, 1945-78

	Percentage of Transfers Via:				
Host Country	Independent Licensees	Minority-owned Affiliates	Majority-owned Affiliates	Wholly-owned Affiliates	Total Number
Canada	5.0%	6.2%	1.1%	87.8%	180
Colombia	7.7	11.5	26.9	53.8	26
Netherlands	10.0	30.0	8.3	51.7	60
Argentina	15.6	17.2	6.3	60.9	64
United Kingdom	17.0	12.9	6.7	63.4	194
Brazil	17.1	6.7	5.7	70.5	105
Australia	17.5	12.6	4.9	65.0	143
Mexico	17.6	30.6	13.9	38.0	108
Italy	23.3	14.4	4.4	57.8	90
France	26.2	5.4	10.0	58.5	130
Spain	26.3	14.1	3.5	56.1	57
Belgium	27.1	5.1	8.5	59.3	59
Germany	30.5	17.9	2.1	49.5	95
Turkey	30.8	38.5	15.4	15.4	13
Sweden	36.8	31.6	0.0	50.0	12
S. Africa	37.5	20.0	0.0	42.5	40
India	41.7	8.3	0.0	50.0	12
Switzerland	41.7	8.3	0.0	50.0	12
Taiwan	44.4	0.0	5.6	50.0	18
Japan	45.9	53.4	0.7	0.0	146
Venezuela	58.3	20.9	0.0	20.8	24
Peru	62.5	25.0	0.0	12.5	8
Other	49.6	10.8	3.3	36.3	240
Total	25.9%	17.1%	5.3%	51.6%	1,843

be preferred in distant and unfamiliar markets. Note that licensing activity among the nations labeled "other" is extremely high. this group includes many secondary markets that may be perceived as more unfamiliar, distant, and risky.

Several other factors can be related to high rates of licensing. In some cases, such as Japan, India, Peru, and Turkey, national regulations discourage or prohibit direct investment and promote licensing as a conscious national policy. The higher rates of licensing in West Germany and other European nations may reflect cross-licensing relationships with large competitors in those nations. Large German and French firms are major parties in such oligopolistic industries as chemicals, aluminum, and electrical apparatus. The presence of these large firms may encourage licensing activity in order to maintain industry stability. This line of reasoning may also explain why the United Kingdom exhibits much higher rates of licensing than Canada.

These international differences in investment and licensing patterns must be kept in mind in analyzing other independent variables. To control for the effects of host country and time on recipient decisions, the dependent variable was redefined. To reflect the effect of country characteristics, a "mean recipient value" was calculated for each country. All transfers were valued as 1 for an independent licensee, 2 for a minority-, 3 for a majority-owned affiliate, and 4 for a wholly-owned subsidiary. These values were summed for all transfers to each country and divided by the number of observations to yield a measure of the relative use of different recipients in each country. Each transfer observation was then normalized by subtracting the mean recipient value for the host country and period of transfer. This adjusted dependent variable was then tested relative to measures of experience and other dependent variables through analysis of variance.

The results (Figure 2-6) show that significant relationships exist between these adjusted rates and various measures of experience. "Spread sequence" below refers to whether an observation is the first, second, third, and so on, transfer for a given product. all four experience variables show a positive and significant relationship with recipient patterns. A positive coefficient in these tests signifies that when the independent variable increases, the type of recipient tends to fall above the mean recipient value for any given country. The dependent variable is ordered such that higher values correspond to greater equity participation and control by the U.S.-based parent. In these tests, increased experience correlates with greater equity participation in initiating foreign manufacturing.

The results of these tests support the proposition that experience has a powerful effect on recipient decisions, just as it influences location, sequence, and timing decisions. Experience, both general and specific, encourages the use of direct investment in initiating foreign manufacturing for U.S. products.

Figure 2-6
A Test of the Relationship between Experience Variables
and Type of Recipient for Individual Transfers, Adjusted for the
Mean Recipient Value of the Respective Host Country:
Results of an Analysis of Variance

Variable	F-statistic	Probability of Significance
Aggregate Prior Transfers	19.3	.01
Prior Transfers in Country	16.1	.01
Prior Transfers in Industry	8.5	.01
Spread Sequence	13.8	.01

The experience factor emerges from these analyses as a powerful variable in explaining the international spread of manufacturing for the sample of products. In addition, a variety of other variables were also tested in the multivariate analyses. A number of these variables also correlate significantly with transfer patterns. In particular, a second set of variables exhibits a powerful relationship with patterns of transfer activity. These variables reflect aspects of a phenomenon that is theoretically related to the experience factor. To introduce this phenomenon, consider the question—why is the distinction between general and specific experience important?

Chapter III

Experience Effects and Company Characteristics

Experience effects will not be realized equally in all transfer decisions. It has already been seen that transfer experience levels for different industries within a firm have a significant relationship with timing and recipient decisions. This trend in itself suggests that experience effects are not fully and equally applicable to all transfer decisions within a given firm. To address this issue, a more precise understanding is needed of how experience is accumulated and utilized within the firm.

A wide variety of experience-related factors can act to reduce the costs of foreign manufacturing. In the host country, use of existing manufacturing facilities, sourcing links, administrative systems, and channels of distribution all provide economies of scale. At the headquarters level, similar economies of scale are derived from the use of manufacturing technology, market research, and administrative systems. Learning benefits can be derived in planning and implementing projects from repetition of tasks at both host and headquarters levels. Information accumulated at both headquarters and host levels can be used to provide more accurate estimates of project costs and revenues, reducing uncertainty about the project.

These general experience benefits may not be equally applicable to all transfer decisions. There are limits to which resources can be applied or transferred within an organization. Human resources in one nation cannot be readily used in others. Market research in one nation cannot be fully utilized in a second country. The international immobility of such resources is obvious. Perhaps as significant is the immobility of resources across industries.

An established distribution network may be of no value to new products in unrelated industries. Also at the host country level, management and manufacturing facilities may be only partially applicable to a new product. Central resources such as market research, advertising, and brand names will not transfer across product lines. Such resource immobility is one reason for distinguishing between general and specific experience. A second reason also emerges from this analysis.

Some companies appear to be better able to apply experience benefits to foreign manufacturing projects than others. Certain firms consistently introduce new products abroad more quickly and extensively than other firms. This ability correlates highly with certain company characteristics. For example the application of experience resources to transfer decisions seems to be more difficult for highly diverse firms.

Product Line Diversity

Firms active in many industries can be expected to exhibit a lower ability to realize experience benefits. The fact that the firm is active in many industries increases the probability that experience resources derived from existing facilities and operations at home and abroad will not be applicable in all transfer decisions. The distinction between general and specific experience becomes more important as the firm becomes more diverse because of resource immobility across industries.

Product diversity exhibits a significant relationship with transfer timing patterns. Firms active in five or less industries initiate foreign manufacturing for their new products significantly faster than more diverse firms. Over 40.0 percent of all new products introduced by less diverse firms are manufactured abroad within three years of U.S. introduction. Firms active in more than 10 industries manufacture only 27.9 percent of their products abroad within three years. As Table 3-1 reveals, transfer ratios and transfer rates are roughly equal regardless of levels of diversity.

These results suggest that diversity inhibits the speed of transfer activity. A further examination suggests this effect may not be due to the limited transferability of resources across industries alone. This point arises in examining transfer activity for products in different industries within the firm.

Products were classified according to their relationship to the firm's principal SIC 3-digit industry. Two categories of products were established— those in the parent's principal industry, and those in other industries. Transfer patterns for these two types of products exhibit a significant trend. Products within the firm's principal industry are manufactured abroad more quickly than products in other industries, regardless of the level of diversity. Transfer ratios and transfer rates are also higher for products within the principal industry. This pattern conforms to expectations. The firm's experience resources will be most highly developed in its principal industry, resulting in more rapid and extensive transfer activity than in other industries.

Table 3-1 suggests that product diversity inhibits transfer activity because experience resources cannot be applied across a wide range of industries. The fundamental immobility of experience benefits will thus result in reduced transfer activity. Since more diverse firms are active in a wider range of industries, their experience resources will be less applicable to all transfer decisions.

TABLE 3-1

Initial Transfer Lag, Transfer Ratio and Average Annual Transfer Rate for 954 Products: By Parent's Number of SIC 3-digit Industries at Time of U.S. Introduction

Parent's Number of Industries	Number of Products	Initial Transfer Lag % First Introduced Abroad in:					Transfer Ratio % Introduced abroad as of 12/77	Average Annual Transfer Rate from Year of First Foreign Production to:	
		One year or less	Two to three years	Four to five years	Six to nine years	Ten or more years		Three years thereafter	1977 year-end
1 to 5 SIC 3-digit Industries	289	23.5%	16.6%	12.1%	12.8%	10.4%	75.4%	.959	.296
6 to 10 SIC 3-digit Industries	440	16.1	12.5	10.9	15.9	22.7	78.1	.951	.311
More than 10 SIC 3-digit Industries	225	14.2	13.7	12.8	14.7	19.1	74.5	.949	.323
Total	954	17.7%	14.1%	11.7%	14.7%	18.1%	76.3%	.952	.308

The results of Table 3-2 suggest that another factor plays a significant role in transfer decisions. Firms active in fewer industries initiate foreign manufacturing more quickly for products within their principal industry than more diverse firms. This implies that differences in transfer timing are not due strictly to the composition of products introduced by the firm. Composition accounts for a significant fraction of the differential in transfer timing patterns evident in Table 3-1, as diverse firms clearly introduce more products outside their principal industry. However, for any given type of product, less diverse firms initiate foreign manufacturing more quickly. This result leads to the contention that differentiation inhibits transfer activity.

Differentiation occurs as firms grow in size and scope.[1] The process of differentiation necessarily results in more indirect and complex communication patterns.[2] The result of this process is a reduced ability to coordinate activities within the firm.[3] Communications can become distorted as messages are transmitted through a larger number of intermediaries, and more management time is consumed in bureaucratic procedure as administrative systems are formalized.[4] In addition, as separate divisional units are formed, the firm's unity of purpose declines. Divisional barriers may limit the firm's ability to apply existing resources to all transfer decisions.[5]

One division may have resources that can provide benefits to a foreign project, for example. If that project stands to benefit only a second division, the first unit may be reluctant to cooperate. If each division limits access to its overhead resources by other divisions, the firm as a whole will not realize its potential experience benefits. Divisionalization creates communication and access barriers that may limit the firm's ability to fully utilize its experience resources. It can be hypothesized that these barriers will be greatest in diverse firms with certain types of organizational structures.

That proposition gains some support from Table 3-2. A similar pattern emerges when product diversity is examined in relation to recipient patterns. Firms active in 10 or more industries use licensing in one-third of all transfers, while firms with 5 or less industries use licensing in 21.8 percent of all transfers, as shown in Table 3-3. Not only do more diverse firms exhibit a higher rate of licensing in total transfers, but they use licensing more frequently for any given type of product. Less diverse firms use licensing significantly less than highly diverse firms within their respective principal industries alone. Since lower licensing levels correlate with greater experience effects, this pattern further supports the proposition that diversity reduces the firm's ability to realize experience effects in transfer decisions.

These tables show that product diversity correlates with slower transfers and a greater use of licensing. The question is, how much of this phenomenon is a function of the fundamental immobility of resources and how much is due to the effects of intangible organizational barriers? The cross-tabulations

TABLE 3-2

Initial Transfer Lag, Transfer Ratio and Average Annual Transfer
Rate for 954 Products: By the Product's Relation to the Parent's
Principal SIC 3-digit Industry and Number of SIC 3-digit Industries

Product's Relation to Parent's Principal Industry and Parent's Number of Industries	Number of Products	Initial Transfer Lag % First Introduced Abroad in:					Transfer Ratio % Introduced abroad as of 12/77	Average Annual Transfer Rate from Year of First Foreign Production to:	
		One year or less	Two to three years	Four to five years	Six to nine years	Ten or more years		Three years thereafter	1977 year-end
Products Within Parent's Principal SIC 3-digit Industry	370	21.9%	16.0%	11.6%	13.0%	14.6%	77.1%	1.066	.319
Number of Industries									
1 to 5	166	27.7	18.7	11.4	10.8	10.8	79.5	1.069	.314
6 to 10	136	16.8	14.6	10.3	16.2	19.8	78.1	1.061	.323
More than 10	68	17.6	11.7	14.7	11.8	13.2	69.1	1.054	.329
Products Within Other Industries	584	15.5	13.0	11.8	15.7	20.4	74.1	.886	.301
Number of Industries									
1 to 5	123	17.9	13.8	12.7	13.0	12.2	69.6	.892	.289
6 to 10	304	15.8	11.8	11.2	16.4	22.7	77.9	.881	.304
More than 10	158	12.7	14.5	12.0	16.4	22.1	77.7	.887	.304
Total	954	17.7%	14.1%	11.7%	14.7%	18.1%	76.3%	.952	.308

TABLE 3-3

Transfers of 580 Products, Classified by Type of
Recipient, Product's Relation to the Parent's Principal
SIC 3-digit Industry and Number of SIC 3-digit Industries

Transfers Classified by Relation of Product to Parent's Principal Industries and Number of Industries	Percentage of Transfers Via:				Total Number of Transfers
	Independent Licensees	Minority-owned Affiliates	Majority-owned Affiliates	Wholly-owned Affiliates	
All Industries					
1 to 5 Industries	21.8%	15.8%	4.5%	57.9%	871
6 to 10 Industries	28.4	17.8	6.0	47.8	747
More than 10 Industries	33.3	17.3	6.2	43.2	225
Within Principal Industry	17.4	17.5	5.1	60.0	749
1 to 5 Industries	15.2	15.7	5.2	63.6	446
6 to 10 Industries	19.6	19.2	4.3	56.9	224
More than 10 Industries	22.8	22.8	6.3	48.1	79
Within Other Industry	31.7	16.8	5.5	45.9	1,094
1 to 5 Industries	28.5	17.2	3.8	50.5	425
6 to 10 Industries	32.3	17.2	6.7	43.8	523
More than 10 Industries	39.1	14.4	6.2	40.3	146
Total	25.9%	17.1%	5.3%	51.6%	1,843

suggest that immobility alone does not explain this finding.

These simple cross-tabulations leave much to be desired, and the skeptical reader should consider this an introductory examination of the issue. At this point, however, the data suggest that product diversity correlates with slower transfer activity and greater use of licensing.

These cross-tabulations are subject to several intervening effects. Most importantly, this discussion implicitly assumes identical experience levels for firms at different levels of diversity. Reduced transfer activity is then associated with the inability of the more diverse firm to fully apply experience benefits to transfer decisions. Obviously, the level of general experience within firms varies considerably. The correlation coefficient between parent's aggregate prior transfers and product diversity is .409 in Appendix I. Consequently, the cross-tabulations above *understate* the significance of the trend toward reduced transfer activity. More diverse firms possess *higher* levels of general experience, but exhibit reduced transfer activity.

Product diversity also correlates highly with time. Since the products appearing in the high diversity categories tend to be more recent, they can be expected to exhibit shorter initial transfer lags, ceteris paribus. When the time factor is normalized, the trend toward reduced transfer activity by more diverse firms becomes even more significant.

Although the correlation between product diversity and reduced transfer activity appears to be significant, the association between product diversity and the existence of internal communication and access barriers is nebulous at best. The existence and effects of these barriers are extremely difficult to establish and test. Additional insight into this issue can be gained, however, by examining the organizational structure of the firm and its relationship to patterns of foreign manufacturing activity.

Organizational Structure

The firm's organizational structure can facilitate or inhibit internal communications and access to resources. Lawrence and Lorsch relate effective internal communication to the firm's ability to "integrate" diverse units within the firm.[6] Structure affects the ability of the firm to integrate its operations.

The creation of separate divisions raises barriers that inhibit communication and access to resources. Some structural forms attempt to facilitate communication and access across these barriers. International divisions, for example, are responsible for transferring expertise from product and functional units into international markets. Such units must communicate across divisional lines to access product and functional resources in other divisions. It can be hypothesized that the existence of an international division will stimulate transfer activity.

For the purposes of this study, six broad types of organizational structures were defined. Firms were then classified into one of these six categories at the time of introduction for each product. Since organizational change was fairly frequent among the firms in this sample, individual firms are represented in a number of categories. The six categories used in this study are:

1. Domestic Functional

    Firms in this category have no formal product divisions or international division. They are divided by functional lines (e.g. production, marketing, finance). International operations in such firms generally report as autonomous units directly to the president.

2. Functional with International Division

    Such firms differ from the above in that a separate unit exists with responsibility for international operations and functions. The head of this unit manages all international operations and functions and reports to the president.

3. Domestic Product

    Firms in this category are broken down into separate divisions based on product lines. Each of these units has control over its domestic market, but has no international operations. International operations tend to be autonomous and report directly to the president.

4. Product with International Division

    This organizational form consists of a number of product divisions responsible for their products in the domestic market, while an international division is responsible for all products in international markets.

5. Global Product

    Individual product divisions in such firms are responsible for their products in both domestic and foreign markets.

6. Global Matrix, and Area

    Responsibilities for individual markets overlap in this organizational form. Generally a product division and an area manager share responsibility for a given market. Functional managers may also be involved. Area structures were included in this category, as they are similar to a matrix organization with a single or few product line dimensions.

Multinational firms typically follow an evolutionary track of organizational development that is depicted graphically in Figure 3-1.

Figure 3-1
Phases of Organizational Structure for 180 U.S.-based
Multinational Enterprises, 1900-78

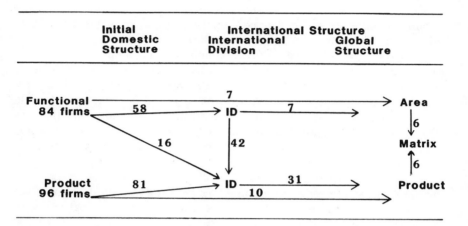

The following organizational structures are represented in the graph:
1) Domestic Functional
2) Functional with International Division
3) Domestic Product
4) Product with International Division
5) Global Product
6) Global Area
7) Matrix

Not pictured on graph: 5 cases from structure 3 to structure 6
                           3 cases from structure 1 to structure 5

Also not pictured: 8 cases of reverse moments

Source: Harvard Multinational Enterprise Project. See also Stopford, J.M. and Wells, L.T., Jr., *Managing the Multinational Enterprise* (New York: Basic Books, 1972)

The "terminal" structures in this chart are global structures based on product divisions, functional or area divisions.[7] The matrix combines these units in a three-dimensional structure. As can be seen, the global product division format has been the most widely adopted global structure.

This pattern reflects many forces, but a common argument for organizing by global product divisions has been to "facilitate technology transfer." The chief executive officer of one firm in this study described the reorganization of their firm along global product lines as a step "to remove the international division as a barrier to the flow of technology." If the reasoning developed above holds, this argument is fallacious. The ability of separate product divisions to pursue international opportunities will be reduced, not enhanced, by elimination of the international division. Divisionalization will reduce communications and result in a lower ability to apply experience resources to all transfer decisions.

Individual divisions within firms organized by global product lines may possess relatively little foreign experience. Other divisions' experience resources will be less accessible in firms organized by global product lines. Higher estimates of foreign manufacturing costs and uncertainty will result, and consequently, less foreign investment activity. To the extent that any division is unable to apply relevant corporate resources to a transfer decision, transfer activity will be reduced. The inability of the firm to share resources and costs across divisions will deter many direct investment projects.

The global matrix form, on the other hand, attempts to facilitate communication and access to resources between relevant product, area, and functional managers for any transfer decision. Access to central and local resources is encouraged by this structure as well. It can be hypothesized that firms organized in a global matrix structure will initiate foreign manufacturing more quickly and extensively than firms organized along global product lines.

These hypotheses can be tested by examining patterns of transfer activity for firms in different organizational structure. Transfer timing patterns vary considerably for firms in different structures.

Several clear trends emerge from Table 3-4. Firms with international divisions consistently manufacture new products abroad more quickly and extensively than firms in domestic functional or product structures. For product and functional firms, the addition of an international division results in an increase in speed, rate, and extent of transfer.

A very striking result is the performance of firms organized along global product lines. Such firms are extremely conservative in initiating foreign manufacturing. In fact, they exhibit longer initial transfer lags than firms organized along domestic product lines. Where 8.1 percent of the global product firms' new products were manufactured abroad within one year, 13.8

TABLE 3-4

Initial Transfer Lag, Transfer Ratio and Average Annual Transfer Rate for 954 Products: By Organizational Structure of Parent at Time of U.S. Introduction

Parent's Organizational Structure	Number of Products	Initial Transfer Lag % First Introduced Abroad in:					Transfer Ratio % Introduced abroad as of 12/77	Average Annual Transfer Rate from Year of First Foreign Production to:	
		One year or less	Two to three years	Four to five years	Six to nine years	Ten or more years		Three years thereafter	1977 year-end
Domestic Product Divisions	128	13.8%	17.8%	8.5%	7.8%	21.2%	69.6%	.846	.261
Domestic Functional Divisions	84	19.1	10.8	12.0	11.9	20.3	73.8	.949	.277
Product with International Division	403	19.6	12.7	13.2	17.4	20.8	81.6	.962	.296
Functional with International Division	93	20.7	14.0	9.7	15.1	12.9	72.1	.979	.298
Global Product Divisions	140	8.1	11.4	10.7	15.7	17.1	64.3	.832	.266
Global Matrix	106	23.6	20.7	13.2	13.2	8.5	85.9	1.189	.426
Total	954	17.7%	14.1%	11.7%	14.7%	18.1%	76.3%	.952	.308

percent of the domestic product firms' new products appear abroad within a year. This trend is even more striking when the considerable time correlation effects in this table are held constant. Note also that the transfer ratio for global product firms is 53.6 percent—an extraordinarily low percentage, although again time correlated. Transfer rates for such firms' products manufactured abroad average only .266 transfers per year in the aggregate, and only .832 transfers in the first three years. Again, this trend is even more striking when adjusted for time effects. There is a very powerful force at work here. Firms organized by global product lines exhibit significantly lower propensities to initiate foreign manufacturing than firms with international divisions. This finding supports the contention that internal communication and access barriers inhibit the application of experience resources to transfer decisions.

The possibility that these results are misleading due to intervening effects must be considered. These trends are strengthened significantly when the time factor is held constant, but are there other factors that should be considered? The one issue that appears significant is the possibility of variance in other parent firm characteristics. Are the firms in this sample which account for the global product observations significantly different from the other firms in the sample? Cluster analysis for a range of company characteristics proved negative. These firms tend to be more diverse, larger, and to have more general experience than other firms, but these characteristics also apply to firms organized by global matrix. To further explore this issue, however, transfer timing patterns for the firms in global product structures were examined in more detail.

Twelve firms introduced products in the U.S. while organized along global product lines. All of these firms remain to this day in the global product structure.

A rather simple test can be conducted by examining transfer timing patterns before and after transition to a global product structure. The results are highly time-correlated, since the global product observations are more recent. Nonetheless, observe in Table 3-5 that these 12 firms actually initiated foreign manufacturing for new products more quickly before they made the transition to a global product structure. Transfer ratios and rates also decline once the firm changes to a global product structure.

These findings suggest the importance of internal communications and access to experience resources. The presence of an international division facilitates these processes. With such a structure, experience resources relevant to foreign manufacturing accrue within one unit of the organization. These resources can be readily accessed and utilized in transfer decisions. The international division can also combine projects from different product areas to realize economies that individual divisions could not.

TABLE 3-5

Initial Transfer Lags, Transfer Ratios and Average Annual Transfer Rates for
Products Introduced by 12 Firms: Classified by Whether Firm was
Organized by Global Product Divisions or Another Structure at
Time of Product's U.S. Introduction

Parent's Organizational Structure	Number of Products	Initial Transfer Lag % First Introduced Abroad in:					Transfer Ratio % Introduced abroad as of 12/77	Average Annual Transfer Rate from Year of First Foreign Production to:	
		One year or less	Two to three years	Four to five years	Six to nine years	Ten or more years		Three years thereafter	1977 year-end
Global Product Divisions	140	8.1%	11.4%	10.7%	15.7%	17.1%	63.0%	.832	.266
Other	101	13.9	13.9	11.9	14.9	29.8	84.4	.921	.296
Total	241	10.5%	12.4%	11.2%	15.4%	22.5%	72.0%	.869	.278

A Behavioral View

Behavioral theories of management emphasize the effects of personal management values and characteristics on decision-making. A wide body of literature describes how such factors affect corporate decision-making.[8] Such factors will also be important in transfer decisions.

The personal characteristics of the managers responsible for transfer decisions are likely to vary considerably in different organizational structures. Managers within an international division will hold different attitudes about foreign manufacturing than managers of global product divisions. Global divisions are often run by former domestic division managers. These individuals are likely to exhibit a preference for domestic operations as a reaction to uncertainty about foreign operations. When such managers assume control for international operations, transfer activity may revert to the risk-averse patterns common in the early stages of foreign expansion. On the other hand, international division managers naturally emphasize foreign opportunities relative to domestic projects.

Such factors may contribute to the observation that transfer patterns for global product division firms closely resemble those of domestically organized firms. Firms with international divisions exhibit higher levels of transfer activity than global product division firms.

The behavioral view cannot as readily explain the difference in transfer patterns between firms organized by global product divisions and those organized by global matrix. There are no significant differences in the characteristics of firms organized by global product lines relative to those organized by a global matrix other than structure. Both types of firms tend to be more diverse, larger, and more experienced than the average firm. Yet, global matrix organizations exhibit significantly higher propensities to manufacture products abroad. Over 44.0 percent of all new products introduced by such firms are manufactured abroad within three years of U.S. introduction. These results are time-correlated, but note that 85.9 percent of all such products have been manufactured abroad by 1978. That ratio, highest among all of the organizational categories, defies the time trend. Transfer rates for products in this category also exceed those of other categories by wide margins.

The matrix organization, because of its less rigid hierarchies and broader communication channels, permits more open discussion of potential projects, which will tend to result in more rational corporate decisions. Matrix organizations stimulate a higher level of interaction among management than global product divisions. Such interaction often occurs in a setting of ambiguous authority relationships. As a result, communication will be more direct and informal. Decisions will be made on the basis of group consensus rather than by an individual manager. Personal biases, and particularly those caused by uncertainty, will have less effect on the decision because of the nature of the decision-making process.

Structure and Licensing Patterns

If organizational structure affects the firm's estimate of foreign manufacturing costs, a correlation between structure and type of recipient patterns can be anticipated. A priori, the presence of an international division should be accompanied by lower rates of licensing, since these firms will be able to apply experience benefits that enhance the economics of direct investment. Firms organized by global matrix structure should exhibit lower rates of licensing than firms organized by global product lines.

Licensing activity does in fact vary significantly according to the

Table 3-6
Transfers of 580 Products, Classified by Parent's
Organizational Structure at Time of U.S. Introduction

Transfers Classified by Organizational Structure	Number of Firms	Number of Products	Number of Transfers	Percentage via Licensees
Domestic Product	14	87	339	33.3%
Domestic Functional	11	103	459	27.4
Product in Int'l. Division	17	215	695	27.8
Function with Int'l. Division	4	54	108	20.4
Global Product	6	49	66	30.3
Global Matrix	4	62	176	5.1
TOTAL		580	1,843	25.9%

organizational structure of the firm. Firms organized by domestic product divisions exhibit the highest rate of licensing. Exactly one-third of all cases of foreign manufacturing for products introduced by such firms are initiated by independent licensees. Functionally organized firms exhibit a significantly lower rate of licensing activity, again supporting the proposition that diversity inhibits foreign manufacturing activity.

The addition of an international division to either of these two structures correlates with a significant drop in licensing activity. Just as firms with international divisions initiated foreign manufacturing in foreign subsidiaries more quickly and extensively, they also exhibit a preference for use of direct investment. These patterns suggest that international divisions increase the firm's ability to apply experience resources to transfer decisions. The more favorable production economics that result stimulate the initiation of manufacturing in foreign subsidiaries.

One of the most striking results in this study is the relative use of licensing by firms in global product and global matrix structures. Over 30.0 percent of all cases of foreign manufacturing for products introduced by global product firms are initiated by independent licensees. Products introduced by global matrix firms spread abroad almost entirely through foreign subsidiary networks. Only 5.1 percent of all cases of foreign manufacturing for such products are initiated by independent licensees. This remarkable divergence in recipient patterns provides further support for the theory that ease of internal communication and access to resources affect transfer decisions.

Organization by global product lines fragments the experience resources of the firm, reducing scale economies and increasing uncertainty, thus lowering motivation for foreign manufacturing activity. Divisionalization also fragments learning curve benefits. Each division will operate under its own learning curve, where a single learning curve with respect to international operations would exist in firms with an international division.

To further test the relationship between organizational structure and transfer patterns, an analysis of variance model was applied to the data. Parent organizational structure was treated as a categorical factor in an analysis of covariance model. The test included as independent covariates the firm's general and specific experience levels relevant to a product, the firm's level of diversity and, as a dummy variable, the relationship of the product to the firm's principal industry. These variables were included so that their effects on transfer timing patterns could be controlled. The dependent variable in this model is initial transfer lag.

The relationship between parent organizational structure and initial transfer lag follows a consistent pattern over time. This relationship is significant at the .001 level for the 1945-77 period, and it is also significant in each of the four cross-sectional subsets of this period in which there were sufficient observations to permit further testing. In each period, products introduced by global matrix firms are manufactured abroad in a foreign subsidiary most quickly. A negative sign in Table 3-7 designates fewer than average years to initial foreign production.

Firms organized by domestic product or function exhibit longer than average initial transfer lags in each period. It is interesting to note that this differential has increased significantly over time. The addition of an international division again correlates with faster initiation of foreign manufacturing.

The results here moderate the patterns that appear in the simple cross-tabulations. Functionally organized firms do not exhibit shorter initial transfer lags than firms organized by product in this test. Firms organized by global product divisions introduce products abroad more quickly than either domestic product or functional firms. Much of this deviation is due to the adjustments taken into account for diversity, size, and experience levels. Functionally organized firms tend to be smaller, less diverse, and less experienced than firms organized by product line; both are much less so than global product firms. However, global product firms do exhibit longer lags than firms with an international division. In a similar test using transfer rate as a dependent variable, a consistent pattern emerged. Functional firms again exhibit lower transfer rates than product firms, with or without an international division. Global product firms exhibit lower transfer rates than product firms with an international division. The primary patterns—the positive influence of the international division and the remarkable distinction between global matrix and global product firms—appears even more significant in this second test. A positive sign indicates above average transfer rates in Table 3-8.

These tests control for the experience level of the firm, time, the firm's diversity, and a product's relation to the parent's principal industry. The remaining variances in initial transfer lags and transfer rates are highly significant. What explains this variance? Its existence is strong evidence that the ability of the firm to realize experience efforts in transfer decisions is significantly affected by its organizational structure.

TABLE 3-7

Adjusted Deviation from Mean Initial Transfer Lag for
Period: By Time Period and Six Organizational Structure Categories

Organizational Structure Category	Period of U.S. Introduction					
	1946–50	1951–55	1956–60	1961–65	1966–70	1971–77
Domestic Product Division	*	*	1.72	.26	5.42	7.35
Domestic Functional Divisions			1.23	4.67	6.63	11.26
Product with International Division			−2.55	−1.24	−1.63	.05
Functional with International Division			− .45	−2.59	−1.13	1.32
Global Product Division			1.80	2.70	−1.84	−1.56
Global Matrix			−3.64	−3.96	−4.52	−2.46
Factor F-Ratio			6.9	12.6	23.1	11.2
Significance			.001	.001	.001	.001

Note: Deviations are adjusted for effects of other independent variables: Parent's
       aggregate number of prior transfers at time of product's U.S. industry,
       Number of SIC 3-digit industries, and product's relation to parent's principal
       SIC 3-digit industry.

*No observations in Global Product or Matrix categories.

Table 3-8
Adjusted Deviation from Mean Transfer Rate
for Six Organizational Structures

Organizational Structure Category	1945-77
Domestic Product Division	-5.07
Domestic Functional Divisions	-6.85
Domestic Product with International Division	3.39
Domestic Functional with International Division	-4.56
Global Product	2.86
Global Matrix	11.28
Factor F-Ratio	5.9
Significance Level	.001

Chapter IV

Technology and Competition: A Rival Hypothesis

Increased experience has been presented as the principal cause of acceleration in foreign manufacturing activity. A rival hypothesis can be posed, however.

Competition for foreign markets has risen steadily in the postwar period. New competitors have emerged from several quarters. First, more and more U.S.-based firms have ventured abroad. In 1950, 81 U.S.-based firms owned manufacturing subsidiaries in six or more nations. By 1967 there were 187 such firms, and 254 U.S.-based firms manufactured in six or more nations in 1975.[1] These firms have also diversified their foreign operations into an increasingly broad range of industries. In 1950, U.S. multinational firms were active abroad in an average of four SIC 3-digit industries. In 1975, the average number of industries for each multinational had risen to 11.[2] In addition to newcomers from the U.S., new rivals from Europe,[3] Japan,[4] and elsewhere[5] have appeared on the scene. The result—increasing competition for global markets—can have an important impact on transfer decisions.

The Effects of Competition

Rising competition can be expected to have three principal effects on transfer patterns. First, rising competition can stimulate transfer activity. The threat of competition in an export market can serve as the trigger for foreign investment, according to the product cycle model.[6] When such threats emerge more quickly because of rising competition, it can be expected that foreign manufacturing will be initiated more quickly. If so, initial transfer lags will shorten, and transfer rates will increase, as observed in this study.

A second effect can also be expected. Rising competition will discourage foreign investment in product lines which do not impart significant advantages to the firm. Foreign investment activity in marginal product lines can be expected to decline.

Third, licensing activity can be expected to increase as competition rises. Firms compare returns from exports, foreign investment, and licensing in exploiting a product overseas. If the first option is effectively closed and the second viewed less favorably because of rising competition, licensing will increase in importance.

This reasoning leads to three propositions about the effects of competition on transfer activity. As the competitive leads of U.S. firms diminish, those products that spread abroad via direct investment will do so more quickly. However, if U.S. firms perceive themselves to be less able to compete abroad, fewer products will be produced in foreign subsidiaries. Licensing activity will increase as returns from foreign investment decline.

In order to examine these propositions, an understanding of the nature of competitive leads is required. Competitive leads are often spoken of as barriers to entry or oligopoly factors. These factors play a dominant role in foreign investment theory. Hymer proposed that oligopoly power is a necessary condition for foreign investment.[7] The sources of such power are diverse.

Caves emphasizes marketing strength based on differentiated products.[8] As seen in Chapter I, access to cheap capital stimulates direct investment. Control of markets, either for inputs or final products, also supports foreign investment.[9] Superior management, information, economies of scale, and government aid also provide advantages that support direct investment. Perhaps the most significant source of competitive advantage for U.S.-based firms has been superior technology.

All of these factors are difficult, if not impossible, to measure. Consequently, empirical tests of how levels of competition affect transfer patterns are extremely difficult to devise. In this study an attempt is made to measure the competitive advantage associated with individual products by classifying them in terms of their technological lead. Several variables are employed to measure technological lead. These variables serve as proxies for the level of competition facing the firm.

The Role of Technology

A general definition of technology might include the following elements:

1. Product design and function
2. Production capability
   a. physical equipment—plant and machinery
   b. process configuration—integration of physical equipment
   c. organization of work—integration of labor with physical equipment
   d. know-how—start-up and maintenance ability

Improvements in any of these areas generate competitive advantages.

Improvements in production techniques represent technological advantages, but the principal source of U.S. advantage in many industries has been product innovation. The role of product innovation in international trade and investment has been widely discussed and documented.

The international spread of product innovations has been analyzed by a number of scholars. Some researchers have focused on the spread of innovations in specific industries.[10] Others have analyzed the international diffusion of an individual innovation or of a small number of case studies.[11] Yet another body of research centers on the activities of individual firms in the international spread of innovations.[12] Perhaps the most notable contribution in this area is Vernon's product life cycle model.

This model begins with innovation in the home market. As the new product becomes commercially successful at home, the firm begins to export the product to foreign markets. The model postulates that firms will invariably serve foreign markets through exports in the initial stages of market penetration. Even when economics justify foreign production, firms are unlikely to initiate foreign manufacturing until a strategic motivation appears. In this model, the principal motivation is a threat that the firm's existing foreign market will be lost. The threat arises from the perception of emerging competition in the market, or from barriers created to discourage imports into the market.

In a world of increasing competition, the trend toward faster transfer activity is entirely consistent with this model. Threats to export markets will emerge more quickly as a result of rising competition. It is important to note that rising competition is not limited to basic industries such as steel, automobiles, and chemicals.[13] Serious competition has developed in such high-technology industries as aerospace,[14] nuclear equipment,[15] telecommunications,[16] and consumer electronics.[17]

This increased competition can stimulate the spread of foreign manufacturing in several ways. First, the presence of a technologically-capable national firm in any host country poses a potential threat to export markets in that country. As the gap between a U.S.-based firm and firms in any host country narrows, the magnitude of this threat grows. One result will be more rapid initiation of manufacturing for products which spread to such countries.

The entry of new global competitors in any industry stimulates foreign manufacturing even in host countries which do not possess indigenous abilities in the industry. The presence of these new competitors, who aggressively bid for foreign markets, increases the bargaining power of host countries. The ability of these nations to encourage local manufacturing rises proportionately.

If rising competition stimulates foreign manufacturing activity, it can be hypothesized that highly significant innovations will spread more slowly than other new products which are manufactured abroad. The threat of losing an export market, which triggers foreign investment in the product cycle model, is not likely to occur as soon for significant innovations as other products. The level of technological lead is in effect a measure of the firm's competitive strength.

Significant innovations can be hypothesized to spread abroad more slowly for a second reason. If innovation imparts significant competitive advantages, the innovator will be able to pursue a discriminatory pricing policy to capture consumer surpluses in its markets.[18] This approach initially entails high prices and low volumes and leads to gradually falling prices and rising volume. Rather than entering a new market with a price at which marginal cost equals marginal revenue (P_E), the firm captures consumer surpluses by following a sequential pricing policy from P_1 to P_3. The firm's ability to pursue this strategy will be a function of the size of its technological lead.

Figure 4-1
A Discriminatory Pricing Strategy

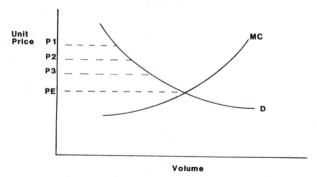

If firms with unique products do pursue such a strategy to maximize profits, the initiation of foreign manufacturing will be postponed. Under such a strategy, it will take longer to reach the market volume necessary to warrant production in the foreign market.

The greater the lead, the greater the ability of the firm to pursue a discriminatory pricing policy in foreign markets. In addition, several other factors suggest that significant innovations will spread abroad more slowly than other products. Consumer resistance, debugging problems, and marketing inefficiencies all restrict the rapid spread of major innovations. These factors slow the rate of adoption of the product in a market. Another set of factors slows the spread of manufacturing. Production techniques are likely to be highly unstable for such products, and technical expertise may be tightly constrained, discouraging foreign production.[19] In addition, the experience resources which stimulate direct investment will not be well-developed for such products.

These factors lead to a hypothesis that foreign manufacturing for significant innovations, e.g. those which embody substantial technological leads, will be initiated by foreign subsidiaries more slowly than for other products which spread abroad. This hypothesis primarily addresses the effects of competition on the international spread of manufacturing for U.S. products. Technological lead can only be defined in terms of the effective level of competition faced by the innovator at any point in time.

This is a difficult variable to quantify. Studies have been conducted that relate patterns of international technology transfer to the number of firms offering a product.[20] However, the international data necessary for such an analysis would be difficult to obtain for such a large sample of products. This study relies on several variables that serve as proxies for levels of technological lead.

The first of these variables is the distinction drawn in this study between innovations and imitations. Each of the 954 new products analyzed in this study is classified as either the first introduction of a particular product or as an imitation of a product first introduced elsewhere after 1945. All 954 products qualify as commercially and technically significant new products. The only distinction is the level of competition faced by the introducing firm. By definition, innovators face less immediate competition than imitators. In relation to the hypothesis above, innovations are expected to spread abroad more slowly than imitations. It can also be hypothesized, however, that a greater percentage of the innovations will be produced abroad in the long run because of the greater competitive advantages they provide. Rising competition will discourage foreign investment by firms with less significant competitive advantages.

In fact, innovations tend to appear abroad as quickly as imitations. Table 4-1 reveals that 18.7 percent of the innovations are produced abroad within one year of U.S. introduction, as compared to 17.1 percent of the imitations.

It is notable that a significantly higher percentage of the innovations have been manufactured abroad by 1978. Innovations also exhibit transfer rates that exceed those for imitations. These findings support the oligopoly theories of international investment. They imply that only the most significant innovations can be exploited effectively abroad. Firms initiate foreign manufacturing for those products in which they can best maintain a competitive advantage. They are less likely to make an investment in products which do not carry as great a competitive edge.

When initial transfer lags are adjusted to reflect the fact that more innovations are produced in foreign subsidiaries than imitations, the speed of initial transfer for the two groups is almost identical. Of those innovations and

TABLE 4-1

Initial Transfer Lag, Transfer Ratio and Average Transfer
Rate for 954 Products: By Whether Introduced as
Innovations or Imitations of Existing Products

| Products Introduced by: | Number of Products | Initial Transfer Lag % First Introduced Abroad in: | | | | | Transfer Ratio | Average Annual Transfer Rate from Year of First Foreign Production to: | |
		One year or less	Two to three years	Four to five years	Six to nine years	Ten or more years	% Introduced abroad as of 12/77	Three years thereafter	1977 year-end
Innovator	406	18.7%	16.3%	11.6%	14.3%	20.2%	81.1%	1.017	.326
Imitator	548	17.1	12.4	11.6	14.4	16.6	72.9	.905	.295
Total	954	17.7%	14.1%	11.7%	14.7%	18.1%	76.3%	.952	.308

imitations that spread abroad, 23.1 percent and 23.4 percent, respectively, first appear abroad within one year of their U.S. introduction.

These results are reinforced by examination of transfer patterns relative to other measures of technological lead. Each innovation was classified as to whether it was considered an "incremental" or "radical" innovation by knowledgeable sources. Radical innovations represent quantum leaps in technology; incremental innovations involve less significant advances, while still involving an extension of technical frontiers. In addition to the hypothesis that firms with substantial leads may postpone foreign production through discriminatory pricing, and that threats to foreign export markets will develop more slowly for such products, one can also hypothesize that radical innovations will involve greater user resistance and debugging problems than incremental innovations. Consequently, these products will spread abroad more slowly than incremental innovations.

Again, however, this reasoning is not supported by the data. Radical innovations spread to foreign subsidiaries as quickly as incremental innovations. As can be seen in Table 4-2, 18.7 percent of the innovations in each group were produced abroad within one year. Radical innovations are more likely to be produced abroad over time, however. Only 76.6 percent of the incremental innovations had been produced abroad by the end of 1977, as compared with 82.6 percent of the radical group. Of those innovations that were produced in foreign subsidiaries, slightly fewer radical innovations spread abroad within one year.

These findings are consistent with transfer patterns exhibited by innovations relative to imitations. In general, the larger the technology lead associated with a new product, the more likely that product will be produced abroad in a subsidiary of the parent firm. This finding supports the oligopoly-based theories of international investment. However, the fact that such products appear abroad as quickly as less significant products does not conform to expectations. Could these patterns be due to intervening effects? Several possible effects deserve examination.

The most obvious question concerns the time distribution of the sample. The tendency for innovations to appear abroad as quickly as imitations could be a result of their more recent introduction. However, as Table 4-3 indicates, the sample of innovations is significantly older than the sample of imitations. This pattern contributes to the higher transfer ratio for innovations, but it only strengthens the impression that innovations appear abroad as rapidly as imitations.

A second possible intervening effect involves the characteristics of the firms in question. Do innovations tend to be introduced by a certain type of firm, while imitations are more common for other firms? Cluster analysis did not reveal any significant distinctions between the two populations. In

TABLE 4-2

Initial Transfer Lag, Transfer Ratio and Average
Transfer Rate for 406 Innovations: By Level of
Technological Advance

Level of Technological Advance	Number of Innovations	Initial Transfer Lag % First Introduced Abroad in:					Transfer Ratio % Introduced abroad as of 12/77	Average Annual Transfer Rate from Year of First Foreign Production to:	
		One year or less	Two to three years	Four to five years	Six to nine years	Ten or more years		Three years thereafter	1977 year-end
Incremental	107	18.7%	14.0%	9.3%	14.0%	20.6%	76.67%	.959	.258
Radical	299	18.7	17.0	12.7	14.4	19.8	82.6	1.038	.351
Total	406	18.7%	16.3%	11.6%	14.3%	20.2%	81.1%	1.017	.326

Table 4-3
Distribution of Innovations and Imitations by Period of U.S. Introduction

Period of U.S. Introduction	*Number of Innovations*	*Percentage of all Innovations*	*Number of Imitations*	*Percentage of all Imitations*
1945-49	99	24.4%	75	13.7%
1950-54	71	17.5	80	14.6
1955-59	75	18.4	78	14.2
1960-64	63	15.5	122	22.3
1965-69	64	15.7	106	19.3
1970-75	34	8.4	87	15.9
TOTAL	406	100.0%	548	100.0%

addition, a test was conducted to compare initial transfer lags and transfer rates, normalized for parent characteristics.

The average initial transfer lag and transfer rate were computed for each parent in the sample. Then, the lag and rate for each innovation and imitation were divided by the average for its parent. The results of this exercise reveal that innovations spread abroad more quickly and rapidly than imitations when compared to average rates for the parent.

Table 4-4
Initial Transfer Lag and Transfer Rate Divided by Parent Average for Innovations and Imitations

Type of New Product	*Number*	*Initial transfer lag as a % of parent average*	*Transfer rate in 3 years following first spread as a % of parent average*
Innovations	406	.969	1.145
Imitations	548	1.024	.892
TOTAL	954	1.000	1.000

A third issue also deserves examination. It has been noted that new products within the parent's principal industry spread to subsidiaries abroad more quickly and rapidly than products in other industries. If firms tend to introduce a larger percentage of innovations within their principal industry, this could result in the patterns above. In fact, the distributions of innovations and imitations are very similar. While 37.4 percent of all innovations are within the parent's principal industry, 39.8 percent of all imitations are within the parent's principal industry. These patterns suggest that intervening efforts do not account for the finding that more technology-intensive products spread abroad as quickly as other products.

The above measures of technological lead focus on individual products. It is important to consider an alternative measure that reflects the technological intensity of firms and industries. A number of studies which analyze the role of technology in international trade and investment focus on research and development spending by firms and industries.[21]

Firms with strong R&D capabilities possess significant competitive advantages. Such firms are able to perceive transfer decisions as one in a series, since new innovations will be generated through ongoing research and development. The prospect of continued innovation provides a strong strategic base and also permits the firm to write off the start-up and overhead costs associated with direct investment over a longer time period and additional products. Firms with lesser R&D capabilities and commitments will be less sure of generating additional new products to exploit overseas.

If R&D-intensity conveys a competitive advantage permitting firms a longer period of grace from competition in foreign markets, R&D-intensive firms can be hypothesized to:

1. introduce a larger percentage of their new products overseas,
2. initiate foreign production more slowly for those products that spread abroad, and
3. make greater use of direct investment relative to licensing in initiating foreign production.

To test these hypotheses, R&D expenditures as a percentage of sales were compiled for each of the firms in the sample. However, measurement of R&D intensity at the level of the firm is not sufficient. It is also important to consider the R&D intensity of the firm's industry. High R&D firms, as measured in absolute percentages, may in fact be spending only at the average rate in their industry. A better measure of the firm's technological advantage will be its rate of R&D spending as a percent of the average rate in its industry.

As Table 4-5 indicates, firms spending more than the industry average on R&D manufacture significantly more of their new products in foreign subsidiaries. Those spending twice the industry R&D rate or more produce 83.8 percent of all new products in at least one foreign subsidiary. Firms spending less than the industry average introduce only 74.1 percent abroad. These results support the first hypothesis above.

TABLE 4-5

Initial Transfer Lag, Transfer Ratio and Average Transfer Rate for 954 Products:
By Parent's R&D Expenditures as a Percentage of Industry Average Rate at
Time of U.S. Introduction

Parent's R&D Expenditures as a % of Sales over Industry Average	Number of Products	Initial Transfer Lag % First Introduced Abroad in:					Transfer Ratio % Introduced abroad as of 12/77	Average Annual Transfer Rate from Year of First Foreign Production to:	
		One year or less	Two to three years	Four to five years	Six to nine years	Ten or more years		Three years thereafter	1977 year-end
Under 100%	395	15.2%	12.2%	11.6%	18.2%	16.9%	74.1%	.593	.294
100 to 200%	299	18.4	15.4	13.4	15.7	14.7	77.6	.812	.296
200% and Over	260	21.5	15.4	10.8	16.5	19.6	83.8	1.501	.338
Total	954	17.7%	14.1%	11.7%	14.7%	18.1%	76.3%	.952	.308

Initial transfer lags do not meet expectations. Firms spending more than the industry average on R&D initiate production in subsidiaries faster than other firms. While firms spending double the industry average introduce 21.5 percent within one year, low R&D firms produce 15.2 percent of their new products in foreign subsidiaries within one year. This finding offers an explanation for the observed tendency of radical innovations to appear abroad as quickly as other products. High-technology firms face favorable foreign manufacturing economics because of their ability to amortize project costs over a longer time period and a larger number of products. Regardless of the cause, however, these data suggest that rising competition cannot effectively explain the acceleration of foreign manufacturing activity. Each variable used to reflect levels of technological lead reveals that, for those products that spread abroad alone, the high-technology products spread abroad more quickly than other products. These findings are based on cross-sectional analysis for various measures of technological lead. In time series, trends in each of these categories show that the speed of transfer for high-technology products relative to other products has generally increased over time. The general impression that competition is not the principal determinant of foreign manufacturing patterns is reinforced by examination of licensing data.

Direct Investment and Licensing
in Exploiting Technology Abroad

Greater competition is hypothesized to result in an increased use of licensing in exploiting new products overseas. The returns and risks associated with foreign investment become less attractive when competition rises. Licensing then becomes relatively more attractive. Absolute returns from licensing can also increase. As foreign firms become increasingly sophisticated, external markets for technology become more efficient, and the value of negotiated agreements with rivals increase.[22]

Where U.S. firms are able to maintain significant barriers to entry, however, licensing activity will not rise as rapidly. This hypothesis is supported by examination of investment and licensing patterns in relation to the firm's R&D-intensity. Firms spending less than their industry average on R&D use independent licensees in initiating over one-third of all cases of foreign manufacturing for their products. Firms spending more than their industry average on R&D use licensing in less than one-quarter of all cases. This pattern is highly consistent with the philosophy espoused by high-technology firms such as IBM in retaining control and ownership of foreign ventures which use the firm's technological resources.[23]

Table 4-6 presents these absolute rates of licensing, but also classifies

TABLE 4-6

Transfers of 580 Products, Classified by Number of Years After
U.S. Introduction, Percentage via Licensees and Parent's
R & D Expenditures as a Percentage of Industry Average
Rate at Time of U.S. Introduction

Products Classified by Parent's R & D Expenditures Rate as a % of Industry Average	Number of Products	Transfers in: Number of Years After U.S. Introduction					Total
		One Year or Less	Two to Three Years	Four to Five Years	Six to Nine Years	Ten or More Years	
Under 100%	241						
Number of Transfers		55	95	88	121	324	683
% Via Licensees		20.0%	32.6%	50.0%	28.1%	33.3%	33.4%
100 to 200%	179						
Number of Transfers		55	67	51	106	301	580
% Via Licensees		16.4%	22.4%	21.6%	21.7%	18.3%	19.5%
200% and Over	160						
Number of Transfers		70	100	60	94	256	580
% Via Licensees		10.0%	17.0%	25.0%	25.5%	28.5%	22.4%
Total	580	180	252	199	331	881	1,843

transfers in terms of the number of years elapsed since a product's U.S. introduction. This is a critical distinction. Note that licensing activity is substantially higher for low R&D firms in the early years of a product's life, while high R&D firms exhibit rising rates of licensing as products age.

This pattern also appears for other variables used as proxies for level of technological lead. A comparison of recipient patterns for innovations and imitations appears in Table 4-7. Although innovations exhibit a higher absolute rate of licensing, the distribution of licensing activity over time varies significantly. Imitations exhibit higher than average rates of licensing in the first five years of their life, while the bulk of licensing activity for innovations occurs later in the product's life. This pattern is consistent with the notion that increased competition stimulates licensing activity. Imitations face immediate competition, while innovators generally benefit from a monopoly position for some time before competition sets in. Higher rates of licensing for innovations later in the product's life can be related to increased competition as the innovation matures.

A U-shaped curve is particularly evident for the innovations in Table 4-7. This trend is pervasive in examination of licensing and investment patterns for innovations. There is a strong tendency for direct investment to account for the bulk of all early transfers for innovations, then to decline sharply to account for approximately half of all transfers for a brief period before rising to a slightly higher rate again.

This pattern may reflect several important processes. First, the age of the product may be the best measure of the firm's technological lead, or competitive advantage. An innovator's market power is greatest during the product's early life. The absence of competition allows the firm to demand the highest possible terms for sale of the technology. If these returns are not available through licensing because of buyer uncertainty, the firm can capture them through direct investment, or simply delay negotiations until a later time.

The increase in licensing activity roughly five years after the U.S. introduction of an innovation may reflect rising competition as well as a reduction in buyer uncertainty. Once competition sets in, transfer activity will increase, as firms hasten to secure returns from foreign markets. In such competitive situations, licensing can be used to close a market to a competitor and generate substantive returns, while entailing little resource cost to the firm. In such situations, the opportunity cost of withholding a license may be nil. Stobaugh has found that licensing activity rises rapidly when competition increases.[24]

The decline in licensing activity following the peak five years after U.S. introduction may reflect the fact that licensing is an option only so long as technology is a barrier to entry. As seen above, licensing rates remain higher

TABLE 4-7

Transfers of 580 Products, Classified by Number of Years After U.S. Introduction, Percentage via Independent Licensees and Whether Product is an Imitation or Innovation

Transfers Classified by Whether Product is an Innovation or Imitation	Number of Products	Transfers in: Number of Years After U.S. Introduction					Total
		One Year or Less	Two to Three Years	Four to Five Years	Six to Nine Years	Ten or More Years	
Innovations	221	70	117	106	140	399	832
% Via Licensees		14.3%	19.7%	50.0%	25.0%	29.1%	28.5%
Imitations	359	110	135	93	191	482	1,011
% Via Licensees		15.5%	29.7%	19.3%	24.1%	24.9%	23.7%
Total	580	180	252	199	331	881	1,843
% Via Licensees		15.0%	25.0%	35.2%	24.5%	26.7%	25.9%

for innovations than imitations in later years, As the technology matures, it becomes more difficult to capitalize in a licensing agreement. Once the technology is fully mature, all licensing and investment activity will cease unless the firm possesses other competitive strengths such as a strong brand name.

Similar patterns emerge from an examination of radical and incremental innovations. Radical innovations exhibit a higher absolute rate of licensing but only as a result of greater licensing activity in later stages of the product's life. These findings generally support the view that increased competition leads to higher rates of licensing. An additional test can provide a further measure of the strength of this effect.

Since the number of global competitors active in most industries has risen over time, it can be expected that licensing activity will increase as well. The data reveal a pattern contrary to expectations, however. The relative use of licensing has declined over time. As Table 4-8 indicates, independent licensees accounted for 32.3 percent of all transfers between 1945-55 but only 21.8 percent of all transfers between 1966-75. If rising competition was the driving force behind increased transfer activity, such patterns would not emerge. This trend raises further questions about the role of competition in transfer decisions.

Table 4-8
Transfers of 580 Products, Classified
by Period of Transfer and Percentage
via Licensees

Period of Transfer	Number of Transfers	% Via Licensees
1945-55	136	32.3%
1956-65	677	31.0
1966-77	1,030	21.8
TOTAL	1,843	25.9%

The overwhelming influence of experience effects can explain why the relative use of licensing has declined over time. It is simply a case of one force dominating another in the net results. The proposition that competition is the principal force behind accelerating foreign production activity does not emerge from these data. The finding that significant innovations spread abroad as quickly as other new products also suggests that competition is not the principal factor in foreign manufacturing trends.

This finding might be attributed to the role of exports in serving foreign markets. Faster transfer for innovations may reflect higher export volume for such products. Numerous studies have found a strong correlation between technology intensity and export rates at the industry level.[25] However, research on diffusion rates suggests that market adoption proceeds more slowly for radical innovations than for less significant new products.[26] As a result, market volume would not grow as quickly for radical innovations.

Another explanation can be developed by arguing that technology is only one of many sources of competitive advantage. Shorter initial transfer lags may reflect the inability of superior technology to offset the absence of other sources of advantage. This explanation would neglect the highly significant correlations between measures of technological lead and those for other aspects of transfer activity, such as transfer ratio and rate. These correlations support the view that technology is a vital oligopoly factor in international investment and licensing activity. If the variables employed here do capture the oligopoly power of technology, the speed with which significant innovations spread abroad occurs because firms choose to utilize this oligopoly power in an aggressive manner.

Firms will not always be defensive or reactive in initiating foreign production. The absence of competition may be as much a stimulus to foreign investment as its presence. The evidence here suggests that firms actively pursue foreign investment opportunities, rather than solely responding to competitive threats.

If defensive investment behavior occurs because of high uncertainty, the reduction of uncertainty may stimulate foreign investment. In addition, the strategic orientation of the firm plays a key role in foreign manufacturing decisions. These propositions are addressed in the following chapter.

Chapter V

Corporate Policy and International Investment

Policy consists of a set of internal objectives, philosophies, and strategies that determine corporate behavior in any given situation. Ironically, these elements of policy can often only be measured in terms of behavioral patterns exhibited by the firm. The problem of measurement remains a critical challenge in deciphering the effects of policy orientation on business behavior.

As a result, theories of foreign investment must either assume a set of objectives, strategies, and philosophies in analyzing patterns of behavior, or infer their nature from observed behavior.[1] In either case, the relationship between behavior and policy variables must be consistent for the theory to hold relevance.

Several theories of foreign investment pass the consistency test. Models that depict foreign investment as an exercise in efficient resource allocation, as a by-product of oligopolistic interaction, a response to market failures, or as a defensive response to competitive threats all meet this criterion. Each model assumes a particular policy orientation that is consistent with observed behavior. However, the policy orientation implicit in each model differs significantly from the other models.

Can a general model of foreign investment be developed that permits the firm to vary in its fundamental policies? Such a "contingency model" would treat corporate policy variables in the same way that diversity, size, and experience are used as independent variables. Initial efforts have been made through detailed case analyses of individual companies.[2] Empirical studies have been hampered by measurement problems.

Experience effects provide an indirect means of exploring the impact of policy orientation on investment behavior. Experience appears to correlate with a shift from defensive to more aggressive investment behavior.

Defensive foreign investment behavior occurs when a threat to an existing market is necessary before the firm will initiate foreign manufacturing.[3] Under this paradigm, the firm will continue to serve the foreign market through exports in the absence of such a threat, regardless of relative production costs. This type of behavior results from the high uncertainty associated with foreign operations.

If uncertainty declines as a result of increased foreign experience, will firms become less defensive in their foreign investment behavior? To address this issue, the role of risk and uncertainty in foreign investment must be developed.

Risk and Uncertainty in International Investment

The distinction between risk and uncertainty is rarely drawn in modern management literature. Both represent expected variance in cost and return estimates, but the source of the variance differs substantially in these two categories. One represents systematic risk derived from identifiable environmental events and trends; the other source of variance is more ambiguous. Systematic risk factors can be related to specific exogenous variables. If future values for those variables could be predetermined, risk could be eliminated. If values for the relevant independent variables are given, the outcome of a project can be precisely determined. Uncertainty, in the Knightian sense,[4] represents variance due to ignorance of the variables and dimensions of risk, of cause and effect relationships, and of the fundamental structure of the operating environment. Firms facing high uncertainty cannot precisely measure outcomes even in the absence of systematic risk. This distinction is very important in assessing international investment behavior.

In the early stages of foreign expansion, firms cannot identify the risks associated with foreign investment. They are ignorant of the variables and dimensions of risk involved in foreign projects. Uncertainty will be more important than systematic risk in such investment decisions.

This distinction is critical in evaluating foreign investment projects. A firm active in a number of industries can adequately estimate risk and return for incremental domestic investments in each product line. These estimates can also be applied to foreign investment projects in these industries. However, the firm's confidence in risk and return estimates will be sharply lower for foreign projects.

Decision theory holds that firms will discount projects with higher uncertainty.[5] As foreign projects are generally perceived as entailing more uncertainty, numerous authorities have advocated the use of "risk premia" in discounting pro forma cash flows of foreign projects.[6] An alternative approach, however, permits a more precise measurement of variance. A comprehensive approach can be developed by using a standard discount rate and comparing all projects in terms of variance and return, regardless of location.

The effects of uncertainty can be incorporated in total variance estimates for projects. For example, managers can be asked to state a measure of their confidence in systematic risk estimates in a range from .01 to .99. The original variance estimate (δ) can then be divided by this confidence measure (C) to yield an adjusted measure of variance (δ/C). These adjusted variances can be plotted and projects compared on an uncertainty-adjusted basis.

These two elements in total variance correspond to risk and uncertainty measures. They can also be thought of as reflecting product and country variance elements. The firm expects certain variance in returns in a given industry (δ), but also recognizes that this will vary by country (C). Consider the effects of high country-related uncertainty under this framework. Imagine two projects in the same industry. Each has similar product-related variance and return estimates, but they are located in different countries. One set of estimates carries .90 country confidence levels, while management holds only a .50 confidence level in the other project. On an adjusted basis, the first project is plotted as return equals 1, variance equals 1.1. The second project is plotted as return equals 1, variance equals 2.0. This example typifies comparisons between similar domestic and foreign projects in a given industry. The effects of uncertainty on project selection are shown graphically in Figure 5-1.

This figure depicts a variance-return indifference curve (I) for the firm in question. Any project above this curve, assuming a constant cost of capital, will be accepted; any project below the curve will be rejected. As seen in Figure 5-1, the domestic project is accepted while the foreign project is rejected because of the effects of uncertainty.

Figure 5-1
The Effects of Uncertainty on Project Selection

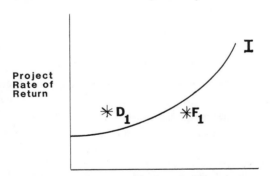

Uncertainty-adjusted variance of project return

This framework is not meant to mirror managerial practice in accounting for risk and uncertainty in project selection. In fact, it begs the question whether the firm should be equally averse to various types of risk. Should the firm equate risk and uncertainty in project evaluations? It does, however, point out the possible effects of uncertainty on foreign project evaluations. The principal difference between foreign and domestic projects will be uncertainty levels.

It can be argued that increased experience will reduce uncertainty levels and stimulate foreign investment activity. If uncertainty is included in variance estimates, and experience serves to reduce uncertainty, valuations of foreign projects can be enhanced as firms gain experience abroad. This process is depicted in Figure 5-2. As foreign experience increases, confidence levels approach those for domestic projects. Assuming foreign project returns and systematic risk levels are in fact similar to domestic estimates, experience enhances foreign projects significantly. The two sets of project evaluations in Figure 5-2 can be attributed to one firm before and after the accumulation of experience, or to two firms in cross-section with different levels of experience. In either case, experience will stimulate foreign investment activity.

Figure 5-2
Risk and Return Estimates for Foreign Projects
as a Function of Experience

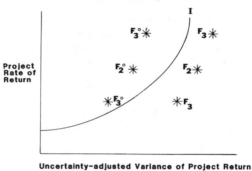

° -evaluations after accumulation of experience

Experience can improve foreign project evaluations, but will it contribute to a reduction in defensive foreign investment behavior? This proposition is difficult to test. The effects of experience on investment behavior can be explored, however, by examining transfer patterns for firms with different experience levels.

It has been shown that firms facing lower levels of competition, as measured by technological lead, initiate foreign manufacturing as quickly as firms facing greater competition. If experience stimulates non-defensive investment behavior, the relative speed of transfer for high-technology products should accelerate as experience rises. Specifically, if experience reduces defensive investment behavior, it can be expected that innovations will spread abroad faster than imitations as experience increases.

As Table 5-1 reveals, widely divergent patterns of transfer activity occur for innovations and imitations at different levels of experience. Imitations spread abroad more quickly, although less often, for inexperienced firms. As

TABLE 5-1

Initial Transfer Lags, Transfer Ratio and Average Transfer Rates for 954 Products:
By Parent's Number of Prior Transfers In Product's Industry for Innovations and Imitations

Parent's Experience Level for Innovations and Imitations	Number of Products	Initial Transfer Lag % First Introduced Abroad in:					Transfer Ratio % Introduced abroad as of 12/77	Average Annual Transfer Rate from Year of First Foreign Production to:	
		One year or less	Two to three years	Four to five years	Six to nine years	Ten or more years		Three years thereafter	1977 year-end
0-2 Prior Transfers									
Innovations	240	12.5%	16.2%	11.3%	17.1%	24.6%	81.7%	.697	.288
Imitations	230	14.3	9.1	11.1	13.5	11.3	59.3	.941	.186
3-10 Prior Transfers									
Innovations	85	25.8	16.5	16.5	16.5	7.9	82.3	1.183	.328
Imitations	90	15.5	22.2	10.0	8.9	23.3	79.9	.753	.286
11 or More Prior Transfers									
Innovations	81	29.6	16.1	7.4	21.0	3.7	77.8	1.833	.441
Imitations	218	21.5	12.8	13.7	13.3	16.6	77.9	.861	.385
Total	954	17.7%	14.1%	11.7%	14.7%	18.1%	76.3%	.952	.308

experience increases, innovations appear abroad more quickly than imitations. This pattern is very significant when adjusted for the percentage of new products in each category that have been introduced abroad. For the most inexperienced firms, 24.1 percent of all imitations which spread abroad do so within one year, while 15.3 percent of the innovations introduced abroad by such firms appear within one year. For firms with extensive experience, the respective rates are 24.4 percent for imitations and 38.0 percent for innovations.

Another powerful pattern is evident in transfer rates for the first three years of transfer activity. For inexperienced firms, imitations spread abroad at an annual rate exceeding rates for innovations by .250 transfers per year. Among highy experienced firms, the reverse is true. Innovations spread abroad at rates exceeding those for imitations by almost 1.00 transfers per year. Experienced firms appear to be significantly less defensive in their transfer decisions. Innovations spread abroad much more quickly than imitations as experience increases. Inexperienced firms exhibit the expected defensive patterns of investment; products facing lower competition spread abroad more slowly. However, the investment behavior of experienced firms is not consistent with a defensive policy orientation.

These findings lead to some generalizations about the role of uncertainty and experience in foreign investment decisions. The level of uncertainty facing the firm is highest when a new product is being introduced into a new market. Such projects are characterized by extremely high levels of uncertainty at both the product and market levels. For the product, there is uncertainty associated with product design and manufacturing process.[7] Production costs and market demand are extremely difficult to predict. In addition, uncertainty surrounding operations in an unfamiliar foreign environment compounds the firm's perception of risk related to the new product. Highly defensive behavior will result. The firm will be less defensive in introducing new products into

Figure 5-3
Level of Uncertainty in Foreign Investment
Decisions as a Function of Product and
Market Characteristics

TYPE OF PRODUCT	TYPE OF MARKET	
	NEW	ESTABLISHED
NEW	HIGH	MEDIUM
ESTABLISHED	MEDIUM	LOW

established markets, or established products into new markets. Strategies for introducing established products in established markets should not be affected materially by uncertainty.

Firms with no international experience face high levels of uncertainty in all foreign projects relative to domestic projects. Until the dimensions of risk for foreign projects become known, the firm can only discount such projects highly to reflect uncertainty about the projects' results. As experience increases, however, revision of project evaluations will permit better estimates of project results. As Figure 5-2 suggested, reductions in uncertainty will cause the firm to view foreign projects more favorably in relation to domestic projects, assuming returns in foreign markets are similar or superior to domestic returns.

Experience will also enhance foreign projects involving significant innovations relative to other foreign projects. Recall that Chapter II examined the country sequence of manufacturing for new products. The approach there was—given a new product, how does the firm assign priorities to a range of foreign markets? The inverse approach is also important —given a foreign market, how are priorities assigned to a range of products?

This process can be viewed in terms of a traditional capital allocation model. A number of project opportunities are analyzed, returns and risks are estimated, and priorities are assigned on the basis of these estimates.

Projects involving new product lines will have several characteristics that distinguish them from other projects, however. New products carry a relatively high degree of uncertainty. Product design is often in a state of flux. Production techniques are subject to radical change. The nature of demand for the product is not fully understood. Faced with these uncertainties, managers will discount projects involving such product lines. This process can be observed in investment patterns.

As we have seen, firms tend to introduce new products initially into similar markets in which they have an established presence. On the other hand, it can be hypothesized that when entering a foreign market for the first time, firms will first introduce those products with which they are most experienced. Such strategies will minimize uncertainty in the market entry.

Such a trend can be observed in the pattern by which product lines are introduced into new markets. Table 5-2 classifies product lines into three types—those within the parent's principal industry, within related sectors, and within other industries. For this table, product line data for 180 U.S. based multinational enterprises are used to provide an extensive view of this phenomenon. The percentages of all first, second, third, and so on, entries into individual markets accounted for by each type of product are tabulated.

Products in the principal industry account for 36.6 percent of all first entries into foreign markets. In other words, the initial product line

TABLE 5-2

SIC 3-digit Product Lines Introduced into Foreign Manufacturing
Subsidiaries by 180 Multinational Enterprises: By Relationship
to Parent's Principal Industry and Sequence of Product Line
Entries into Host Country

Sequence of Product Line Entries into Host Country	Number of Subsidiary Product Lines in:						Total Number
	Same SIC 3-digit as Parent's Principal Industry		Other SIC 3-digit in Parent's Principal 2-digit Industry		Other		
	No.	Percent	No.	Percent	No.	Percent	
First Product Line Entry	1,567	36.6%	1,247	29.1%	1,468	34.3%	4,282
Second Product Line Entry	787	26.4	980	32.8	1,216	40.7	2,983
Third Product Line Entry	361	19.3	606	32.3	907	48.4	1,874
Fourth Product Line Entry	200	15.0	472	35.3	664	49.8	1,336
Fifth Product Line Entry	109	15.5	235	33.3	361	51.2	705
Sixth Product Line Entry	67	13.1	170	33.2	275	53.7	512
Subsequent Product Line	220	14.8	448	30.3	831	55.4	1,499
Total	3,311		4,158		5,722		13,191

introduced into a foreign market came from the firm's principal industry in more than one-third of all cases. However, the principal industry becomes less and less important in subsequent activity in any given country. Other industries account for a rising percentage of later introductions.

This pattern is consistent with the previous analysis of experience factors in location decisions. As noted in the analysis of country manufacturing sequences, firms tend to introduce new products in similar, established markets before venturing into less familiar territory. A similar process appears in the sequence by which products are introduced into a given market. Firms tend to enter markets with products from their principal industry initially and then expand in secondary lines. Once established in the market, additional product entries tend to come from outside the parent's principal industry. This pattern suggests that the importance of product line experience declines as the firm's experience in a given host country increases. If the firm is well established in a particular foreign market, it will be less concerned about uncertainties related to new product lines.

As firms gain more experience overseas, the distinction between established and new product lines will diminish. Just as secondary markets were seen to improve their position in the country manufacturing sequence as a result of increased experience, secondary or more risky product lines will benefit from experience as well. The reduction of general uncertainty levels benefits such projects in the investment selection process.

This process was reflected in Table 5-1 where significant innovations spread abroad more rapidly and extensively than other products as experience increases. It can be demonstrated that valuations of projects involving such innovations are enhanced relative to other projects by experience.

For this proposition to be true, it need only be established that the firm's risk-return indifference curve has a positive slope. If that holds, equal reductions in country-specific uncertainty will benefit projects with high variance more than other projects.

Consider the following example. The firm manufactures two product lines. The first has a variance-return plot of 1, 1; the second a plot of 3, 2 for the domestic market. In evaluating these product lines for introduction into a foreign market, the firm assumes that variance levels abroad are double that for domestic investment. This assumption reflects uncertainty associated with the foreign country. The firm's confidence levels in project estimates are .50 due to country-specific uncertainty. Consequently, in evaluating these foreign projects, the two projects are plotted at 1, 2 (A_1) and 3, 4 (B_1) as in Figure 5-4. After gaining extensive experience in that country, however, the firm's confidence levels in project estimates rises to .90. Its revised project plots then become 1, 1.1 (A_2) and 3, 2.2 (B_2), assuming that the product lines actually had the same potential in the foreign market as at home after all. Project B, involving the more risky product line is now clearly preferred over Project A, the more conservative investment.

Figure 5-4
The Effects of Uncertainty Reduction on Project Priorities

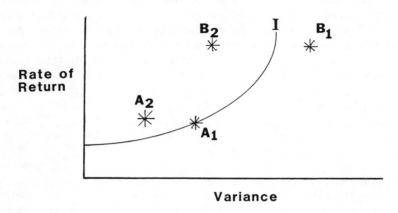

This model can explain why innovations spread abroad more quickly than imitations as experience increases. Reductions in country uncertainty encourage the firm to substitute projects with high variance for projects with lower variance and return. Since such projects frequently involve radical innovations, these products appear abroad more rapidly as experience rises.

The framework used here assumes that there are three basic elements of variance important in project valuations—country uncertainty, product uncertainty, and product/country systematic risk. Experience reduces the importance of product and country uncertainty in project valuations by leading the firm to isolate and measure systematic risk elements specific to a given project. So long as the systematic risk revealed by experience does not exceed the uncertainty removed, experience will stimulate foreign investment.

The firm's estimation of project variance is a function of its experience. This process can have a significant effect on foreign investment activity. However, the manner in which the firm reacts to a given variance also affects foreign investment activity. Some firms are more variance-averse than others.

Variance-Aversion and International Investment

Variance-aversion is an element in the strategic orientation of the firm. Some firms are highly conservative in their attitudes toward variance; others are more aggressive. Figure 5-5 presents variance-return indifference curves for two such firms. These curves, given the firm's cost of capital, reflect the firm's minimum acceptable return at any given level of variance.

The effects of variance-aversion on international investment patterns can be explored in this theoretical situation. Assume the indifference curves represent two firms with identical costs of capital. Furthermore, these two firms appraise the six projects in question identically in terms of variance and return. Despite these similarities, their project selection results will differ substantially as a result of differing attitudes toward variance. Firm one will accept one domestic project (D_1) and two foreign projects (F_1 and F_2), assuming no budget constraints. Firm two will reject all three foreign projects.

Figure 5-5
A Theoretical View of Project Selection Results
for Firms with Different Degrees of Risk-Aversion

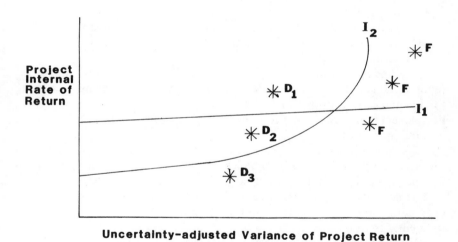

D 1, D 2, D 3 –Domestic Projects
F 1, F 2, F 3 –Foreign Projects

The effects of variance-aversion on foreign investment activity are very difficult to measure. The variable most frequently used as a proxy for variance-aversion is the size of the firm. Larger firms are thought to be less averse because the consequences of failure for a project of given size hold less significance to them than to smaller firms. Larger firms can more readily reduce corporate variance through diversification. For such reasons, Horst cites firm size as the most important determinant of propensity to invest abroad.[8]

If large firms are less variance-averse than small firms, larger size should correlate with greater transfer activity. In order to examine the relationship between size and investment behavior, the firms in this sample were classified into three categories. These categories reflect the ratio of a firm's sales volume to that of the largest U.S. firm in its industry in the year of a product's U.S. introduction. Firms with sales below one-third of the industry leader's sales were classified as small; those between one- and two-thirds were classified as medium; and those over two-thirds appear under the large category. Normalization by industry controls for the varying scale of investment required in different industries.

Contrary to expectations, relative size in an industry correlates inversely with levels of transfer activity. Small firms introduce products abroad more quickly than larger firms. Transfer ratios and three-year transfer rates are also higher for small firms. Table 5-3 reveals that over 20.0 percent of all new products introduced by small firms appear abroad within one year of U.S. introduction. Large firms introduced 16.0 percent of their new products abroad within one year.

Size has also been related to licensing and investment activity. Telesio reports that small firms have a greater propensity to use licensing in entering foreign markets.[9] Stopford and Wells also found that smaller firms were more likely to enter minority joint ventures than larger firms.[10] This proposition can be examined in this study.

The results in Table 5-4 do not support the proposition that smaller firms use licensing more frequently. Smaller firms were found to use licensing in 25.5 percent of their transfers. The largest firms in an industry use licensing in 26.2 percent of all cases of transfer. Although this difference is insignificant, it does not support the proposition that small firms use licensing more frequently than large firms.

These findings do not reject the hypothesis that size and investment activity are positively correlated. They do reveal, however, that this relationship can be overpowered by other factors that influence the strategic orientation of the firm. Are there any reasons to believe that small firms hold different policies towards foreign expansion than large firms?

These results occur because of an overriding bias in this sample of firms. The sample of small firms in this study is dominated by young, aggressive, growth-oriented enterprises. The initial criteria for selection of firms in this study were presence on the 1965 Fortune 500 and foreign manufacturing in six or more countries. These criteria insure that a large percentage of the observations for small firms apply to aggressive, internationally-oriented

TABLE 5-3

Initial Transfer Lags, Transfer Ratios and Transfer Rates for 954
Products: By Parent's Size Within its Principal Industry 1/

Parent's Size in its Principal Industry	Number of Products	Initial Transfer Lag % First Introduced Abroad in:					Transfer Ratio % Introduced abroad as of 12/77	Average Annual Transfer Rate from Year of First Foreign Production to:	
		One year or less	Two to three years	Four to five years	Six to nine years	Ten or more years		Three years thereafter	1977 year-end
Small	464	20.1%	14.9%	14.0%	15.7%	15.7%	80.4%	1.005	.302
Medium	196	15.3	11.2	8.7	12.2	23.5	71.0	.873	.278
Large	294	16.0	14.6	10.2	13.6	18.7	73.1	.924	.338
Total	954	17.7%	14.1%	11.7%	14.7%	18.1%	76.3%	.952	.308

1/ Small firms are those whose sales volume was less than one-third of the largest firms
in its principal industry in the year of a product's U.S. introduction. Large firms
are those with sales exceeding two-thirds of the industry's largest firm.

TABLE 5-4

Transfers of 580 Products: Classified by Number of Years after U.S. Introduction, Percentage via Licensees and Parent Size at Time of U.S. Introduction

Parent Size in Industry	Number of Products	Transfer in: Number of Years After U.S. Introduction					Total
		One Year or Less	Two to Three Years	Four to Five Years	Six to Nine Years	Ten or More Years	
Small	312						
Number of Transfers		74	116	107	178	513	988
% Via Licensees		14.9%	34.5%	39.3%	23.0%	23.0%	25.5%
Medium	105						
Number of Transfers		40	38	28	46	57	209
% Via Licensees		27.5%	18.4%	32.1%	30.4%	26.3%	26.8%
Large	163						
Number of Transfers		66	98	64	107	311	646
% Via Licensees		7.6%	16.3%	29.7%	24.3%	33.1%	26.2%
Total	580	180	252	199	331	881	1,843
% Via Licensees							25.9%

Note: Size in industry was calculated by dividing the firm sales by the largest firm in the industry. Those with less than one-third the leader's sales were classified as small; those with more than two-thirds of the leader's sales were classified as large in the industry.

firms. The policy orientation of these firms contribute to the observed difference in transfer activity.

These findings only serve to point out that differences in policy orientation can overpower the established relationship between size and propensity to invest abroad. Other factors besides the size of the firm dictate its attitudes toward variance. Experience factors play an important role in determining corporate attitudes toward variance. Other factors developed in innovation research, behavioral studies, and industrial organization theory also influence attitude toward risk.

The ability of size to reflect variance-aversion has been debated elsewhere. Although Schumpeter held that only large firms could risk uncertain investments in developing new products,[11] other scholars hold opposing views. Williamson notes there is an equally strong argument that small firms are more likely to be innovative than larger firms.[12] Theories of organizational development suggest that entrepreneurial activity declines as firms become larger and more formally structured. Two of the characteristics of the transition from a stage 1 to a stage 2 firm are increased size and a change from an entrepreneurial to a more static managerial approach.[13]

Large firms may also be more reluctant to introduce innovations, since they will suffer the greatest cannibalization effects when existing products are replaced. Large firms generally have a strong interest in preserving the status quo in an industry. Sultan has shown how such considerations affected decisions to introduce new products in the electrical equipment industry.[14] He concludes that larger firms are unlikely to introduce new products unless the introduction serves to discipline and stabilize the industry. Such motives also appear to have been important in the introduction of the System 370 by IBM in the early 1970s and again in the introduction of the 4300 series in 1979.[15] Smaller firms on the other hand, are much more concerned with speed of entry into a new field because they fear preemption by larger competitors.[16]

One explanation of the patterns found here can be drawn from the theory of oligopolistic imitation. Note that large firms exceed medium-sized firms in rate and speed of transfer. If the large firms are the established dominant firms, the medium-sized firms are the disciplined followers of the dominant oligopolists. The small firms represent aggressive, undisciplined newcomers in the industry.

The medium and large firms are more apt to exhibit the oligopolistic patterns of investment behavior cited by Knickerbocker.[17] Knickerbocker's work reveals a powerful propensity for firms in certain industries to invest abroad as a reaction to competitors' foreign activities. This "follow-the-leader" syndrome occurs most frequently in highly concentrated industries. The clustering of foreign investment in time and space occurs as a result of a strategic drive for competitive stability.

The excursion of one firm into new markets creates the possibility that it might derive a competitive advantage from that new venture. To limit this from occurring, competitors maintain a similar business profile by matching the leader's move. Followers rarely initiate this process for fear of punitive reprisals by the dominant firm. Newcomers are more likely to disrupt established patterns.

The effect of such oligopoly factors cannot readily be tested. The firm's sensitivity to such industrial organization concerns is yet another intangible element in corporate policy that has only been measured in terms of behavior itself.

The policy orientation of the firm is extremely difficult to measure. More effective, independent measures of basic corporate policy variables are needed. Size does not provide an effective measure of variance-aversion. It is unlikely that industry concentration will provide significant measure of sensitivity to oligopoly factors, nor will organizational structure necessarily measure the entrepreneurial spirit of a firm.

In the absence of effective measures, foreign investment theory will continue to be fragmented into overlapping but distinct paradigms, each with a unique assumption about the policy orientation of the firm. A partial step toward unifying these theories can be achieved, however.

Experience levels provide an alternative means of representing corporate policy orientation. Experience can be used to represent the policy orientation of the firm, which will then allow an independent observer to predict which model of foreign investment behavior is most relevant to the firm. In this way, experience variables provide a linkage between the various theories of foreign investment, and a first step in the construction of a unified model.

Chapter VI

Experience Factors in Theory and Public Policy

The effects of experience on foreign investment patterns can be incorporated readily into existing theories of foreign investment. Theories that emphasize relative production costs or financial motives for direct investment are strengthened by inclusion of experience effects. Experience effects can overpower other more visible determinants of investment activity in these models. Internal cost reductions achieved as a result of experience effects can offset environmental trends which discourage foreign investment activity.

These internal firm-specific cost reductions can be incorporated in the financial models of foreign investment. Although finance theories do not emphasize firm-specific factors as determinants of foreign investment, they do recognize the existence of inter-firm variances in project valuations. Experience effects contribute to such variances.

The effects of uncertainty reduction on investment decisions are also important. These effects are developed in Bayesian decision theory. Revision of project estimates through posterior analysis will affect future decisions significantly.[1] The value of incremental information, which is equivalent to reduced uncertainty, also is recognized in Bayesian decision theory.[2] These concepts can be applied as readily to a set of firms in cross-section as to one firm in time series.

Experience can also be incorporated into the oligopoly-based theories of foreign investment. The central proposition of such theories is that market power is a prerequisite to foreign investment. Experience provides a source of such market power. Clearly, experience can never be generated unless the firm originally possesses another source of competitive advantage. However, even after all other competitive leads have vanished, experience can provide the cost advantages and strategic strengths that stimulate direct investment.

Experience plays a further role in theories that emphasize market failure as a stimulus to direct investment.[3] Experience will enable the firm to recognize and measure market failures more precisely, and may raise the firm's propensity to internalize transactions.

The effects of experience on foreign investment patterns can be most readily incorporated into the product cycle model. In comparison to other models of foreign investment, this model is highly specific in orientation.

Individual firms, products, and markets are the units of analysis in this paradigm. Because of this specificity, it offers the richest base for elaboration of the effects of experience on foreign investment.

An Experience Dimension in the Product Cycle Model

The product cycle paradigm cannot be applied to all foreign investment activity. The model assumes that exports precede the initiation of manufacturing in a market. In some cases, notably for export plant location decisions, an entirely different analytical framework is needed. The product cycle model also does not apply to investment activity related to the internalization of international sourcing. A second assumption is that foreign investment involves the extension of a U.S. product line into a foreign market. This is not the case in foreign acquisition activity, although Dubin shows that prospects for introducing additional product lines represent an important consideration in evaluating acquisition candidates.[4]

Observation of investment patterns related to these types of activity has led to questions about the ability of the product cycle model to describe foreign investment behavior.[5] In response, it should be noted that the product cycle model applies to only a certain subset of foreign investment decisions. This paradigm models management decisions to manufacture a product developed in the firm's home market in a foreign nation in order to serve that market. This process is not the sole focus of the model. It also draws the distinction between the international diffusion of a product and the spread of manufacturing for it; provides a normative framework for exploiting innovations overseas; describes international trade flows and industrial organization in a dynamic model; and provides a basis for understanding the effects of oligopolistic interaction on investment decisions. In terms of foreign direct investment activity, however, it applies primarily to decisions to manufacture a new product in a foreign market in order to serve that market.

This type of decision accounts for a majority of foreign investment activity. As noted earlier, the extension of U.S. product lines into foreign markets accounts for 65.0 percent of all cases of U.S. foreign investment, as measured by product line units. That percentage is rising over time. In addition, over 90.0 percent of all foreign manufacturing subsidiaries realize the majority of their sales volume from the market in which they are located.[6] The model applies to the majority of foreign investment decisions. The question is, of course, how effective is it doing so? With slight modification, it appears to represent the decision process for these investment activities very effectively.

The most significant shortcoming of the existing model is the assumption that the firm is defensive in orientation. The possibility of departure from this assumption has been cited by Vernon and Wells.[7] Other orientations can be accommodated within the model, however. The firm's strategic orientation toward foreign investment can be treated as a variable in the model.[8]

A number of factors influence the firm's strategic orientation toward foreign investment. This study establishes the importance of experience factors. The behavior of the firm will be a function of its experience. At one end of the spectrum, inexperienced firms will exhibit highly defensive, reactive behavior patterns. At the other end of the spectrum, firms with extensive experience will exhibit behavior derived from a continuous, efficient scanning for global investment opportunities. Experience levels can be used as proxies for the strategic orientation of the firm toward foreign investment. This element can be incorporated into the product cycle paradigm to model and predict foreign direct investment patterns.

The continued relevance of the product cycle model depends, in the end, on corporate behavior in a rapidly changing world. Recent shifts in the world environment have had a severe impact on U.S.-based multinationals. Although rising experience reduces uncertainty levels faced by U.S.-based firms, a range of environmental factors has raised dramatic uncertainties regarding international investment. The strategic orientation and behavior of multinational firms will be affected by these environmental conditions.

Floating, volatile exchange rates raise uncertainty levels for firms engaged in international transactions. In such an environment, it is virtually impossible to effectively evaluate costs and returns for alternative means of serving foreign markets. Uncertainty regarding such costs will promote defensive investment behavior.

The political environment also appears to be increasingly hostile and unstable. Multinational firms often find themselves the victims of political events. Nationalization and re-contracting of existing investments raise uncertainties about returns from foreign investment.[9]

Rising competition, often from state-supported rivals, also looms as a negative factor in the environment.[10] Many firms have divested significant foreign operations because of deteriorating performance.[11] Such divestments will affect perceptions of future foreign investment opportunities.

Faced with such an international environment, many multinational firms are re-assessing their policies for foreign operations.[12] In doing so, full attention must be given to the experience resources of the firm.

Experience Resources and Corporate Policy

It is widely recognized that foreign sales account for a significant and growing percentage of total sales for many U.S. manufacturing companies. Despite this rapid foreign expansion, there is growing sentiment that foreign growth prospects for U.S. firms are now more limited.[13] Recent trends in foreign investment indicate that U.S. expansion into foreign markets has slowed. New U.S. capital investment abroad, which does not include funds raised or reinvested by existing foreign subsidiaries, has actually declined in the last decade, from $1.6 billion in 1966 to $1.3 billion in 1975.[14] Expressed in constant dollars, the trend is more striking—$1.6 billion vs. $.7 billion. The rate at which new foreign subsidiaries are acquired or created also experienced a dramatic decline in the last decade. The 180 largest U.S. multinational corporations formed or acquired 343 new manufacturing subsidiaries in 1966 as compared with 204 in 1975. At the same time, the number of withdrawals from existing operations increased from 53 in 1966 to 114 in 1975.[15]

In addition to an increasingly difficult international environment, innovation activity appears to have declined. Although measures of research output are difficult to construct, research and development spending by U.S. industry has not kept pace with inflation or sales growth.[16] In addition, many firms have cut back on basic research and focused on refinement of existing products.[17] Many observers believe that the U.S. has lost its lead in industrial research and development.[18]

Faced with a possible decline in the introduction of significant innovations at home, and an increasingly difficult international environment, corporate managers should be concerned about their prospects for the future. What are possible sources of growth for the future?

Existing foreign affiliates represent perhaps the most important source of future growth for U.S. multinational firms. The international expansion of existing foreign susbsidiaries offers the brightest prospects for growth.

Multinational enterprises have made substantial investments in developing channels of distribution, manufacturing facilities, and local management expertise in foreign countries. These investments represent important resources that can be utilized to promote further foreign expansion. They also represent overhead that must be absorbed. Multinational firms can utilize the capacity of their established international systems to best advantage by introducing additional complementary product lines into existing subsidiaries.

In fact, recent trends indicate that this already has become a very important source of growth for multinational firms. While expansion via new subsidiaries has slowed dramatically in the last decade, existing subsidiaries have introduced new product lines at an accelerating pace.[19] Such a strategy permits full utilization of existing resources and generates economies of scale.

In an increasingly uncertain world, expansion of existing operations could become the dominant type of foreign investment activity. A high degree of general uncertainty in the environment, be it due to volatile exchange rates or political tensions, will cause firms to behave more defensively in all investment decisions. The effect will likely be greatest in new areas. Projects in less familiar areas, bearing high degrees of uncertainty, will be affected proportionately more by a general decline in corporate confidence.

Assuming continued high levels of uncertainty in the international environment, several other hypotheses regarding foreign investment patterns can be developed. The first is that the overall level of foreign investment activity by U.S.-based firms will decline. Second, licensing will be used to a greater extent, particularly in unfamiliar areas.

This view, however, neglects one critical factor. Many firms now possess highly-trained managers, fully-developed administrative systems and staff, global subsidiary networks and the ability to recognize and pursue foreign opportunities. These experience resources can be used to generate economies of scale and learning benefits that significantly enhance returns from foreign investment.

Firms that utilize experience resources to effectively exploit innovations in global markets will realize returns that can be used to support further research and development.[20] A strategy that emphasizes R&D and global exploitation of experience resources may be the best response to the current international business environment.

The success of such a strategy depends on the firm's ability to apply experience resources to transfer decisions. Many firms are structured in a way that limits the efficient utilization of experience resources. Organization by global product divisions inhibits the firm's ability to exploit innovations overseas.

Such structures have evolved in part because of the growing use of business planning systems that use planning units defined in terms of product groupings.[21] This trend forces the firm toward structures based on product divisions. The justifications for adopting such systems are not being questioned here. However, for firms whose strategy emphasizes the global exploitation of technology, product division structures are inappropriate.

An issue for conjecture at this point is the relative ability of foreign-based firms to utilize experience resources. Do communications patterns in such enterprises parallel those in U.S.-based firms? In particular, is there as strong an emphasis on communications channels between headquarters and the peripheral units of the system, or are such channels more highly developed in foreign firms?

As foreign firms gain experience overseas, the advantage of U.S.-based firms will decline. Efficiency in the use of experience resources will become all the more important. There is no indication that foreign firms will be more or less efficient in utilizing experience resources. However, such firms may tend to organize along different structures than U.S.-based firms. The emphasis on product divisions will likely not be as strong for such firms. This is an area for further study.

Public Policy Issues

Governments at home and abroad are becoming increasingly involved in the world economy. Many of their actions and policies are aimed at controlling and exploiting multinational enterprises.

The international operations of U.S. corporations have been the focus of lengthy public debate. One of the principal issues in this debate is the role of multinational enterprises in the international spread of technology.

The attention devoted to this phenomenon can be related to something more fundamental—the interests of domestic and foreign groups in productive employment, growth, taxes, exports and import substitution. International manufacturing decisions directly affect each of these goals. Multinational firms, as international manufacturing agents, find themselves caught between the conflicting interests of home and host countries.

Official concern over international technological issues has existed for centuries. The British embargo on textile machinery exports in the eighteenth century represents an early attempt to restrict technology transfer.[22] By the mid-twentieth century, Britain and the rest of Europe found themselves in the reverse situation. European concern over the "technology gap" reflected a desire to acquire U.S. technology.

As U.S. investment reduced the technology gap, a new concern arose in Europe. Many were now troubled because the technologically advanced sectors of European industry were dominated by U.S. subsidiaries. Servan-Schreiber's *American Challenge* is representative of this sentiment.[23] This issue becomes even more important in the less developed countries.

Representatives of the less-developed countries have tended to speak less in terms of technology gaps and have addressed what they consider technological monopolies or oligopolies controlled by firms in the industrial nations.[24] Almost all of the less-developed countries consider technology transfer vital to economic development, but there is common concern about the various costs of acquiring it. Many of these nations, in response to a recent colonial past and desire for economic independence, view foreign direct investment in a negative light. Conflicts over ownership frequently dominate negotiations for technological resources.[25] The Japanese model, with its controls on direct investment and emphasis on acquiring technology through licensing, has become increasingly popular in the developing world.

Firms that invest abroad find the governments of host nations directly involved in the market place. This involvement includes government purchases, subsidization or direct control of local competitors, import restrictions, controls on foreign-source investment, and expropriation of local subsidiaries. Negotiated settlements with host governments are essential to success in such an environment. Such settlements often entail local access to the technological resources of the multinational firm.

In managing a firm's technological resources, managers must be concerned about host governments' policies, but they cannot neglect the role of the U.S. government. Within the United States, two basic positions with respect to international technology transfer can be discerned. The first is that generally associated with the labor unions. Charging that international technology transfer reduces U.S. exports and employment, labor has supported attempts to restrict technology transfer and its carrier, foreign investment.[26] The Burke-Hartke Bill was one notable effort toward this objective.[27]

There are also those who perceive technology transfer and foreign investment as beneficial to U.S. interests. Such benefits would include higher returns on capital, secondary exports and increased white-collar employment in administration, consulting, and engineering.[28] Others emphasize the advantages of free trade and recognition that technology transfer is a two-way street.[29] The arguments between those opposed to foreign investment and technology transfer and those in favor are long, complicated and highly politicized.

In formulating policy in this area, several considerations should be kept in mind. Regardless of the objectives of public policy, the costs and benefits of international operations by U.S.-based firms should be understood.

Efforts to develop the welfare implications of foreign investment have been unsatisfying. Many questions remain. This study will not attempt to address them. However, one fact can be established. Foreign governments are extremely active in this area. They play a major role in foreign investment and technology transfer decisions. These governments believe that intervention in the decision process can further their objectives. Since some aspects of international manufacturing resemble a zero-sum game, their benefits may represent cost to the United States. It can be argued, for example, that the more rapid spread of manufacturing for significant innovations occurs because of major incentives and threats applied to foreign manufacturing decisions for these products.

Attempts to limit the use of incentives to influence manufacturing location decisions have been partially successful. The recently completed Geneva round of GATT negotiations included a landmark agreement that limits the use of such incentives. At the same time, however, European governments were aggressively bidding for a new Ford car plant.[30]

U.S. policy in this area has emphasized the importance of international agreements to control government intervention in manufacturing location decisions. On occasion, however, the government has itself intervened in such decisions.[31] Intervention of this sort can lead to confrontations with foreign governments. These confrontations may be indirect, in that multinational enterprises will serve as a buffer between the opposing interests.[32] United States interests, although not yet clearly defined, can be served by such actions. Nonetheless, an active policy by the U.S. would end all pretense of a progressive, cooperative world economic order. This could result in a return to the international economic warfare displayed in the 1930s, albeit with different weapons. This risk must be incorporated into public policy planning.

In considering the implications of an active policy, a prisoner's dilemma framework is appropriate. If the choices are to pursue a laissez faire or an interventionist policy, the outcome is dependent on the choice of other governments. If other governments consistently choose to intervene under the assumption of a laissez faire policy on the part of the U.S., an interventionist approach, or the threat of intervention, can yield positive results. The U.S. can lend discipline and stability to the world economy through a judicious interventionist policy. The form of intervention, through restrictions or incentives, is also important. The history of U.S. policy suggests that incentives would be more consistent with stated objectives and philosophy. The focus of the policy, however, must be on the decision process of the multinational enterprise. Only by understanding this decision process can a national technology policy be developed that furthers U.S. interests.

Appendix I

Correlation Matrix

Variable	1	2	3	4	5	6	7	8	9	10
1. Parent's Aggregate Prior Transfers		.498	.269	.409	.492	.006	.191	.022	.698	.719
2. Parent's Prior Transfers in Product's Industry			.248	.049	.067	-.037	.035	.067	.427	.458
3. Parent's Percentage of Sales Abroad				.007	.618	-.237	.306	.240	.423	.551
4. Parent's Number of SIC's					.597	.257	-.211	.001	.326	.379
5. Parent Organizational Structure						.093	.486	.125	.042	.643
6. Parent Size in Fortune 500							.65	-.114	-.090	-.193
7. Parent Size in its Principal Industry								-.205	.048	.113
8. Parent's R&D Expenditures									.115	.232
9. Year of Product's U.S. Introduction										-.087
10. Year of Transfer										

Appendix II

Description of Data Bases

The data bases used in this study were compiled by the Harvard Multinational Enterprise Project under the direction of Professor Raymond Vernon. Two distinct sets of data are employed.

The first set, described thoroughly in a project publication,[1] includes records for more than 7,000 foreign manufacturing subsidiaries of 180 large U.S.-based multinational enterprises. Variables covering the product lines manufactured by these subsidiaries hold particular relevance to this study. A number of issues can be addressed by tracing the overseas spread of these product lines to foreign manufacturing subsidiaries. Questions of the level, timing, and location of such spread can be addressed, and patterns of spread for these product lines can be related to characteristics of different industries, parents, and host countries.

There are shortcomings to this approach, however. The unit of analysis is measured at the level of SIC 3-digit industries. The use of such broad classifications poses serious limits to analysis and inference. One 3-digit industry may include a wide range of diverse products. One observation in such an industry may actually cover a series of foreign manufacturing decisions for quite distinct products. Also, these data apply only to the use of direct investment as a channel for the international spread of manufacturing for U.S. products.

In order to gain a more precise and comprehensive picture of the international spread of manufacturing for U.S. products, a second data base was developed under the auspices of the National Science Foundation. This data base focuses on a sample of individual new products introduced in the U.S. since 1945. It includes information on almost 1,000 significant new products introduced by a sample of 57 U.S.-based firms.[2]

This second data base offers several advantages. Individual products are narrowly defined, thus avoiding the problems associated with SIC 3-digit classifications. For each product, data are provided for all cases of foreign manufacturing initiated by affiliates or independent licensees of the U.S. firm. In addition, the data base is designed to measure in a general manner the level of technology implicit in each product. This data base includes both new significant technical advances and imitations of such products that have been commercially successful in the U.S. market.

The Company Sample

Data on the development and international spread of individual new products were compiled for 57 U.S.-based multinational enterprises. These firms were selected in a two-step process from the Harvard Multinational Enterprise Project sample of 180 firms.

Initially, a list of 90 firms was developed to provide maximum representation across a range of firm characteristics, including size, foreign experience, product diversity, industry, and R&D intensity. Omitted from the sample were food, beverage, petroleum and cosmetic firms. These industries were excluded because of difficulties associated with the identification of significant technological advances. Drugs were excluded because U.S. regulations on the introduction of such products have had major effects upon the choice of production sites. Military equipment was also excluded.

Of the initial 90 firms, 44 agreed to cooperate in the study. To achieve the desired coverage, 13 additional firms from the group of 180 were added to the sample. The final sample of 57 firms appears below.

The New Product Sample

From annual reports and other public sources, a list of all new products introduced since 1945 was developed for each of the 57 firms. These lists were then reviewed with representatives of the respective firms, as well as other knowledgeable sources, to assess the commercial and technical significance of each product. Firms were asked to classify each product by its cumulative sales to 1976, distinguishing those with sales up to $1 million, those with $1 million to $10 million in sales, and those with $10 million or more in sales. Firms also were asked to reply to the following question: "As a technical development, how would you rate the product in terms of its impact on the market?", and were offered a choice of "major," "minor," or "hard to appraise."

The assessment of technical significance was based partly on information provided by representatives of the 57 firms, and partly on outside sources, including industry trade and technical journals, and knowledgeable sources.

Classification of new products as innovations or imitations also involved some reliance on information provided by parent firms. Most classifications were verified by outside sources. In several cases, more than one firm was listed as the innovator for one product. As an example, the first synthetic rubber compounds were developed jointly and introduced simultaneously by the major tire companies in 1945.

Innovations included in the study were those that satisfied two criteria: they were classified as "major from a technical viewpoint"; and they were reported with cumulative sales of $1 million or more. (In fact, most innovations in the sample had sales of $10 million or more.) Imitations included in the study were those classified as "major" from a technical viewpoint, with sales of $10 million or more.

From an original list of 3,000 new products, 406 innovations and 548 imitations were identified that met the criteria. These new products were then studied in depth to provide data on international spread.

Licensing Data

In addition to examining the international spread of production via the foreign subsidiaries of the firms covered in the sample, this study attempted to shed light on the role of licensing in transferring production capabilities to independent foreign firms. For the purposes of this study, transfers were classified as via license only when the licensor held less than a 5 percent equity participation in the foreign recipient. Data on licensing activity were provided by 32 of the 57 firms in the sample. These 32 firms are denoted in the list of firms by an asterisk.

List of Firms

Addressograph-Multigraph
    Corporation
Allis-Chalmers Manufacturing
    Company*
Armstrong Cork Company*

Borg-Warner Corporation*
Burlington Industries,
    Incorporated

Carborundum Company
Caterpillar Tractor Company*
Chemetron Corporation*
Chrysler Corporation
Clark Equipment Company*
Combustion Engineering,
    Incorporated*
Continental Can Company*
Corning Glass Works
Crane Company

Deere & Company*
Dow Chemical Company*
E.I. du Pont de Nemours
    & Company

Litton Industries, Incorporated

P.R. Mallory & Company
    Incorporated
Maremont Corporation*
Minnesota Mining and
    Manufacturing Company
Monsanto Company

Norton Company

Olin Corporation*
Owens-Corning Fiberglas
    Corporation*
Owens-Illinois, Incorporated*

Pennwalt Corporation*
PPG Industries*
H.K. Porter Company,
    Incorporated*

Raytheon Company*
RCA Corporation*
Rohm & Haas Company

SCM Corporation

Eaton Corporation*

FMC Corporation*
Firestone Tire & Rubber
    Company
Ford Motor Company
Fruehauf Corporation*

GTE
Gillette Company*
B.F. Goodrich Company
The Goodyear Tire & Rubber
    Company

Hercules, Incorporated
Honeywell, Incorporated
Hoover Company*

Ingersoll-Rand Company*
International Harvester
    Company*
International Paper Company

Scott Paper Company*
Singer Company*
Sperry Rand Corporation
Studebaker-Worthington,
    Incorporated*
Sunbeam Corporation

TRW Incorporated*
Timken Company

UNIROYAL, Incorporated*

Westinghouse Electric
    Corporation*

Description of Variables

Data was recorded for 3,577 cases of foreign transfer of production capability. For each of these cases, 54 primary variables were recorded. An additional set of variables was created by transformation or combination of these basic variables. Also, by using a compatible coding system, it was possible to directly reference data on individual parent firms and foreign subsidiaries from the Harvard U.S. Multinational Enterprise Data Base.

Most of these variables classify the transfer according to parent, product, or industry characteristics at the time of U.S. introduction for the product. Other characteristics, primarily those related to the host country, are classified as of the year of transfer. In classifying variables according to such characteristics, assignments in some cases were based on the closest reference year. For most parent and industry variables, data were compiled on an annual basis; for several, at five-year intervals, and in a few limited cases, at longer intervals.

The following list presents the major variables used in this study.

List of Variables

Variable Name   *Description*

PARENT   The firm responsible for introducing the
                new product

PRODUCT   Coded for an individual innovation or
                     imitation

INOVYR   Year of U.S. introduction

SIC   SIC 4-digit industrial classification for
                     the product

SECTOR   Consumer, intermediate or industrial product

LEADIMIT   Innovation or imitation

INCREMENT   Radical or incremental innovation

SPREDEN   Spread categories at entry (licensee,
                     minority-owned, co-owned, majority-owned
                     or wholly-owned subsidiary)

SPREDLT   Spread categories (most recent—used only
                     if different from Spreden)

SUB   Subsidiary code (permits retrieval of
                     subsidiary data from Harvard United States
                     Multinational Enterprise Project data
                     banks)

NATSPRED   Recipient host country

YRSPRED   Year of transfer

DEATH   If production ceased by recipient, method
                     (sub sold, sub liquidated, product line
                     sold or liquidated, license terminated)

YRDEATH   Year of above

PSALE1   Size of parent relative to Fortune 500
                     (Parent sales/sales of 500th firm)

PSALE2   Size of parent relative to industry leader
                     (parent sales/leader sales)

PSKMAJ	Parent's principal SIC 3-digit industry (industries with largest share of parent's total sales)
PSICNUM	The number of SIC 3-digit industries in which the parent manufactured at the time of U.S. introduction for a new product
PRAND	Parent's R&D expenditures/parent sales at time of product's U.S. introduction
PORGAN	Parent's organizational classification at time of U.S. introduction
PNOFSOBS	Parent's number of foreign manufacturing subsidiaries at time of U.S. introduction
PFORSALE	Percentage of parent's sales from foreign sources at time of U.S. introduction (exports from U.S. plus sales of foreign affiliates)
INDRAND	Total industry R&D expenditures/total industry sales at time of U.S. introduction
INDCONC	Percentage of U.S. industry shipments accounted for by four largest firms at time of U.S. introduction
INDLABOR	U.S. labor costs as a percentage of industry shipments at time of U.S. introduction
INDEXPOR	U.S. exports as a percentage of industry shipments at time of U.S. introduction
NATGNP	Host countries GNP at time of transfer
NATGNPER	Host countries GNP per capita at time of transfer
NATLOCAT	Host countries geographic proximity (bordering, w. hemisphere, other)

NATCULT   Host countries cultural proximity (combina-
               tion of English, Latin-based or other
               language and western or other religions)

PTCNTRY   Parent's number of prior transfers to host
               country at time of transfer

PTSIC   Parent's number of prior transfers in product's
               industry at time of U.S. introduction

PTPARENT   Parent's number of prior transfers in all
               industries at time of U.S. introduction

Appendix III

Statistical Tests of Experience Effects and Timing Patterns

A binary logit model was employed to test the relationship between measures of experience and the probability that a given product had been manufactured abroad by 1978. The binary dependent variable was set equal to zero for products that had not been produced abroad; those that had were assigned the value 1.

The results of the test for the entire 1945-77 period show that prior transfers are significantly related to the distribution of this dependent variable. Both measures of experience exhibit a positive and significant relationship with probability of transfer. The higher the number of prior transfers, the greater the probability that the product will be manufactured abroad, ceteris paribus.

Table A
A Test of the Relationship between Experience Variables and the Probability that a Product will be Manufactured in a Foreign Subsidiary: Results of a Binary Logit Analysis

Variable	Coefficient	F-statistic	Level of Significance*
Parent's Aggregate Prior Transfers	.42	12.1	.01
Parent's Transfers in Product's Industry	.51	4.3	.04

$$*V_1 = 1 \quad V_2 = 953$$

These results are subject to time-correlated intervening effects. In order to control for the effect of time, a similar test was run for products introduced in each five-year period since 1945. The results of this cross-sectional analysis, while not as significant as those derived from time-series tests, show a positive relationship between prior transfers and probability of foreign manufacturing for a new product.

Table B
A Test of the Relationship between Experience Variables and the Probability that a Product will be Manufactured in a Foreign Subsidiary: Results of a Cross-Sectional Analysis of a Variance

Variable	Period of U.S. Introduction					
	1946-50	1951-55	1956-60	1961-65	1966-70	1971-75
Parent's Aggregate Transfers						
Level of Significance for F-statistic	.05	.12	.04	.19	.04	.01
Parent's Transfers in Product's Industry						
Level of Significance for F-statistic	.05	.29	.37	.01	.09	.08

Tests were also conducted to examine the relationship between these measures of experience and average annual transfer rates. Analysis of variance was used to test the relationship between these independent variables and transfer rate. The results of these tests were quite significant at both the time-series and cross-sectional levels.

In the test for the entire 1945-77 period, aggregate prior transfers exhibits a very high F-statistic of 158.2. Transfers in the product's industry is also significant at the .01 level. The positive relationship of these variables to transfer rates generally holds in cross-sectional analysis as seen in Figure 2-7.

A similar relationship is exhibited between prior transfers and initial transfer lags. Analysis of initial transfer lags over the entire 1945-77 period reveals that parents' aggregate transfers exhibits an F-statistic of 41.2 and parents' transfers in the product's industry an F-statistic of 21.7 in analysis of variance tests. Both are highly significant in time-series analysis. Both prior transfers variables exhibit generally significant relationships with initial transfer lag in cross-sectional analysis. The coefficients are negative in this case because greater experience results in shorter initial transfer lags.

Table C
A Test of the Relationship between Experience Variables and Transfer Rate
for a New Product: Results of a Cross-Sectional Analysis of Variance

Variable	Period of U.S. Introduction					
	1946-50	1951-55	1956-60	1961-65	1966-70	1971-75
Parent's Aggregate Transfers						
Level of Significance	.20	.27	.01	.01	.01	.38
Parent's Transfers in Product's Industry						
Level of Significance	.12	.33	.01	.01	.01	-.68

Table D
A Test of the Relationship between Experience Variables and Initial
Transfer Lags for New Products: Results of a Cross-Sectional Analysis
of Variance

Variable	Period of Transfer					
	1946-50	1951-55	1956-60	1961-65	1966-70	1971-75
Parent's Aggregate Transfers						
Level of Significance	-.19	-.15	-.10	-.01	-.01	-.01
Parent's Transfers in Product's Industry						
Level of Significance	-.01	-.01	-.01	.99	.11	-.01

Appendix IV
Entry Frequencies in Time Series

APPENDIX TABLE IV-1

Frequency by which 57 U.S.-based Multinational Enterprises Initiated Manufacturing for 325 Individual Products in Country A before Country B, 1945–54

Country A	1	2	3	4	5	6	7	8	9	10	11	12	13	14	15	16	17	18	19	20
										Country B										
1. Canada		.550	.653	.667	.750	.803	.828	.783	.859	.934	.902	.905	.862	.903	.932	.950	.983	1.00	1.00	1.00
2. U.K.			.614	.708	.697	.769	.825	.803	.852	.864	.852	.900	.839	.933	.898	.931	1.00	1.00	1.00	1.00
3. Australia				.606	.603	.656	.655	.717	.733	.852	.774	.821	.800	.923	.860	.904	.980	1.00	1.00	1.00
4. Brazil					.567	.593	.593	.596	.736	.854	.717	.774	.691	.788	.813	.891	1.00	.978	1.00	1.00
5. France						.526	.625	.623	.706	.705	.771	.739	.745	.744	.833	.854	.974	.974	1.00	1.00
6. Mexico							.542	.618	.667	.773	.700	.729	.696	.884	.814	.907	.905	.976	1.00	1.00
7. W. Germany								.505	.512	.634	.571	.571	.619	.686	.697	.750	.964	.964	1.00	1.00
8. Japan									.596	.625	.659	.681	.707	.705	.750	.897	.895	.973	1.00	1.00
9. Colombia										.538	.537	.585	.590	.629	.655	.806	.833	.964	1.00	1.00
10. S. Africa											.511	.541	.543	.618	.655	.741	.880	.957	1.00	1.00
11. Italy												.529	.556	.594	.677	.750	.808	1.00	1.00	1.00
12. Spain													.514	.545	.643	.731	.808	1.00	1.00	1.00
13. Belgium														.531	.615	.731	.760	1.00	1.00	1.00
14. Argentina															.625	.708	.857	.947	1.00	1.00
15. Netherlands																.556	.625	.909	1.00	1.00
16. India																	.571	.889	1.00	1.00
17. Philippines																		.857	1.00	1.00
18. S. Korea																			1.00	1.00
19. Ireland																				1.00
20. Taiwan																				

APPENDIX IV-2

Frequency by which 57 U.S.-based Multinational Enterprises Initiated Manufacturing
for 338 Individual Products in Country A before Country B, 1955-64

Country A	1	2	3	4	5	6	7	8	9	Country B 10	11	12	13	14	15	16	17	18	19	20
1. U.K.		.522	.698	.708	.710	.700	.767	.803	.788	.824	.855	.886	.861	.916	.917	.916	.949	.971	.994	.994
2. Canada			.627	.663	.639	.653	.749	.757	.749	.860	.777	.827	.833	.923	.905	.906	.973	.983	.993	.993
3. Australia				.528	.500	.541	.623	.654	.671	.717	.697	.769	.771	.876	.849	.891	.921	.943	.991	.993
4. Japan					.520	.528	.589	.644	.627	.725	.773	.730	.761	.805	.826	.844	.948	.957	.991	.991
5. France						.525	.590	.649	.651	.690	.709	.763	.772	.852	.881	.880	.922	.964	.981	.991
6. Mexico							.587	.644	.600	.690	.701	.773	.798	.813	.849	.852	.955	.955	1.00	.991
7. W. Germany								.553	.500	.632	.628	.616	.667	.760	.760	.773	.897	.917	.987	.979
8. Italy									.504	.561	.575	.621	.638	.728	.807	.818	.892	.919	.986	.987
9. Brazil										.603	.619	.652	.694	.733	.794	.800	.892	.933	.981	.988
10. Netherlands											.511	.521	.557	.623	.681	.850	.981	.911	.981	.987
11. Belgium												.505	.533	.625	.658	.671	.833	.860	.961	.980
12. Colombia													.590	.618	.725	.696	.841	.869	.939	.961
13. Spain														.573	.636	.631	.849	.870	1.00	.979
14. S. Africa															.509	.547	.773	.829	.966	.971
15. Argentina																.522	.737	.824	.939	.966
16. India																	.714	.750	.922	.964
17. Philippines																		.556	.909	.900
18. S. Korea																			.889	.889
19. Ireland																				.500
20. Taiwan																				

Table IV-3

Frequency by which 57 U.S.-based Multinational Enterprises Initiated Manufacturing for 291 Individual Products in Country A Before Country B, 1965-75

Country A	Country B																			
	1	2	3	4	5	6	7	8	9	10	11	12	13	14	15	16	17	18	19	20
1. Canada		.507	.574	.599	.640	.639	.645	.699	.730	.748	.846	.891	.876	.877	.903	.917	.961	.976	.976	.976
2. U.K.			.571	.612	.629	.632	.673	.702	.734	.732	.835	.860	.881	.899	.885	.929	.959	.975	.983	.983
3. Australia				.539	.558	.575	.580	.651	.672	.681	.810	.839	.851	.851	.868	.851	.952	.970	.980	.980
4. Japan					.503	.514	.541	.611	.643	.656	.769	.827	.814	.851	.851	.896	.945	.966	.966	.966
5. W. Germany						.517	.556	.616	.645	.633	.798	.804	.840	.859	.837	.907	.946	.963	.975	.963
6. France							.510	.598	.605	.628	.755	.815	.822	.833	.835	.882	.938	.962	.974	.962
7. Brazil								.579	.597	.619	.762	.796	.814	.840	.839	.889	.941	.964	.976	.976
8. Italy									.525	.530	.692	.764	.743	.753	.783	.824	.918	.949	.966	.949
9. Mexico										.521	.680	.739	.754	.754	.778	.831	.909	.962	.962	.962
10. Belgium											.657	.681	.706	.712	.750	.787	.904	.941	.941	.960
11. Netherlands												.532	.543	.568	.634	.703	.839	.897	.897	.929
12. Spain													.524	.512	.556	.600	.808	.880	.880	.880
13. Colombia														.514	.568	.656	.840	.876	.875	.913
14. S. Africa															.559	.606	.792	.870	.909	.909
15. Philippines																.571	.762	.842	.842	.842
16. Argentina																	.778	.824	.824	.875
17. Taiwan																		.714	.625	.625
18. S. Korea																			.500	.500
19. India																				.500
20. Ireland																				

Appendix V

Conditional Entry Frequencies

Table V-2 corresponds to the PN table. It is presented in its entirety because it does not share the property that $A_{ij} + A_{ji} = 1.00$. This reflects the manner in which the conditional entry frequencies are defined. When manufacturing is initiated in one country, the country-row increments based on that observation are encoded with a P or N, depending on whether or not the firm was present in that country at the time manufacturing was initiated. Then, each of the other 19 countries are encoded with a P or N for the year manufacturing was initiated in the first country. This determines which of the four conditions apply to a country-row observation.

If a product is produced in an N country before a P country, that observation is not posted to the inverse cell in the PN matrix. It is posted to the inverse cell in the NP matrix, because the country in which manufacturing first occurs determines the first letter of the two letter code. Consequently, $A_{jiPN} + A_{jiNP} = 1.00$.

Whenever the firm is present in only one country of a pair, and manufacturing is initiated in one of the two countries, the observation will be posted either to A_{ij} in the PN table if manufacturing was initiated first in the country in which the firm is present, or to A_{ji} in the NP table if to the other country. The PN table should be interpreted as follows: whenever the firm was present in Country A but not Country B, .xxx of all products introduced into either of the two countries appear in Country A first. The remainder went to Country B first.

Since the NP matrix is the unitary inverse of the PN table, it is not presented here.

Table V-1

Frequency by which 57 U.S.-based Multinational Enterprises Initiated Manufacturing for 954 New Products in Country A before Country B when the Firm had no Prior Manufacturing Experience in either Nation (NN)

Country A	1	2	3	4	5	6	7	8	9	10	11	12	13	14	15	16	17	18	19	20
1. Canada		.671	.885	.883	.772	.892	.895	.972	.958	.932	.930	.959	.875	.945	.944	.958	1.00	1.00	1.00	1.00
2. U.K.			.636	.671	.615	.681	.878	.800	.904	.847	.826	.865	.900	.870	.870	.903	.986	1.00	1.00	1.00
3. Mexico				.548	.553	.594	.560	.691	.841	.769	.746	.938	.815	.797	.833	.881	.955	1.00	1.00	1.00
4. Brazil					.514	.536	.530	.621	.667	.738	.738	.763	.763	.774	.810	.797	.966	1.00	1.00	1.00
5. W. Germany						.558	.597	.641	.632	.719	.692	.677	.727	.828	.758	.818	.984	.953	.967	.950
6. France							.523	.625	.662	.688	.719	.810	.762	.785	.780	.855	.933	.894	.984	1.00
7. Australia								.667	.627	.662	.609	.743	.739	.750	.766	.842	.951	.912	.984	.984
8. Colombia									.603	.738	.577	.673	.608	.596	.694	.704	.929	.870	1.00	1.00
9. Spain										.500	.558	.667	.574	.559	.636	.737	.981	.875	.964	.944
10. Japan											.526	.610	.684	.641	.709	.732	.943	.942	.981	.981
11. Italy												.604	.564	.528	.646	.689	.900	.949	1.000	.974
12. Argentina													.574	.509	.543	.628	.914	.865	.912	.941
13. Belgium														.508	.622	.523	.872	.786	.943	.943
14. S. Africa															.604	.611	.951	.736	.886	.886
15. Netherlands																.583	.920	.639	.958	.920
16. India																	.857	.714	.923	.960
17. Ireland																		.660	.667	.600
18. Philippines																			.773	.750
19. S. Korea																				.555
20. Taiwan																				

Table V-2

Frequency by which 57 U.S.-based Multinational Enterprises Initiated Manufacturing for 954 New Products in Country A before Country B when the Firm had Prior Manufacturing Experience in Country A but none in Country B

Country A	1	2	3	4	5	6	7	8	9	10	11	12	13	14	15	16	17	18	19	20
										Country B										
1. Australia	.000	.333	.798	.586	.935	.788	.649	.881	.543	.736	.906	.872	.989	.286	.776	.864	.940	.931	.679	.970
2. Canada	.799	.000	.936	.774	.941	.913	.884	.936	.802	.846	.878	.970	.992	.703	.845	.941	.983	.877	.877	.904
3. S. Africa	.182	.667	.000	.111	1.000	.700	.250	.692	.250	.545	.667	.824	.909	.143	.474	.875	.857	1.000	.611	1.000
4. Mexico	.568	.833	.825	.000	.739	.818	.667	.827	.550	.755	.811	.877	1.000	.320	.714	.882	.969	.982	.691	.963
5. Argentina	.455	.000	.556	.400	.000	.869	.000	.522	.571	.278	.615	.889	.957	.286	.550	.632	.724	.920	.273	.909
6. Colombia	.350	.500	.800	.200	.758	.000	.348	.614	.222	.621	.640	.816	.921	.182	.526	.905	.889	.949	.433	.911
7. Brazil	.469	.667	.779	.409	.839	.756	.000	.821	.556	.571	.676	.900	.977	.335	.707	.905	.910	.977	.569	.944
8. Belgium	.632	.500	.784	.231	.909	.650	.333	.030	.438	.412	.944	.727	1.000	.333	.606	.846	.857	.950	.500	.925
9. France	.515	.500	.785	.524	.820	.850	.593	.624	.000	.600	.775	.839	.989	.500	.702	.857	.916	.959	.648	.916
10. W. Germany	.708	.556	.836	.750	.951	.788	.722	.848	.731	.000	.833	.948	.990	.542	.815	.902	.894	.982	.710	.982
11. Italy	.500	.333	.886	.462	.778	.846	.600	.882	.636	.607	.000	.911	.967	.133	.500	.851	.850	.967	.536	.934
12. Netherlands	.313	.750	.720	.167	.727	.714	.556	.833	.400	.200	.833	.000	.972	.000	.516	.647	.862	.950	.286	.925
13. Ireland	.000	****	1.000	****	1.000	1.000	****	.500	.000	1.000	1.000	****	.000	****	1.000	1.000	1.000	.750	.000	.750
14. U.K.	.740	.684	.894	.658	.904	.852	.788	.875	.690	.778	.852	.942	.983	.000	.832	.922	.942	.994	.800	.977
15. Spain	.435	.400	.806	.667	.818	.933	.500	.871	.350	.696	.789	.943	.942	.800	.000	.758	.873	.980	.645	.950
16. India	.267	.333	.773	.333	.867	.917	.333	.529	.636	.615	.625	.857	.909	.333	.647	.000	.773	.958	.417	.826
17. Philippines	.000	1.000	****	1.000	****	****	****	1.000	****	.000	.000	1.000	1.000	****	.400	.000	.000	1.000	.000	1.000
18. Taiwan	****	****	1.000	****	.500	****	****	****	****	.000	.000	****	1.000	****	1.000	1.000	.500	.000	.000	1.000
19. Japan	.522	.778	.800	.455	.911	.833	.471	.796	.560	.710	.724	.891	.987	.500	.822	.860	.900	.977	.000	.987
20. S. Korea	.000	****	1.000	****	****	****	****	.000	****	.000	.724	****	1.000	****	.000	.000	.500	1.000	1.000	.000

Countries are not listed in descending priority, but in the standard order used for subtraction of matrices.

**** Frequencies not compiled for country pairs with less than 10 observations.

$Fi_j + Fj_{ji} = 1.0$

Because of the specifications of conditions, $Fi_{j_{PN}} + Fi_{j_{NP}} = 1.0$

The NP table is not presented, but can be developed from the complete PN table above.

Table V-3

Frequency by which 57 U.S.-based Multinational Enterprises Initiated Manufacturing
for 954 New Products in Country A before Country B when the Firm
had Prior Manufacturing Experience in Both Nations (PP)

Country B

Country A	1	2	3	4	5	6	7	8	9	10	11	12	13	14	15	16	17	18	19	20
1. Canada		**.560**	.647	.663	.671	.695	.645	.707	.690	.782	.759	.707	.707	.733	.871	.827	.738	.939	.688	.714
2. UK			**.556**	.595	.648	.639	.593	.650	.673	.585	.375	.678	.712	.816	.844	.829	.667	.969	.800	.917
3. W. Germany				**.550**	.512	.508	.505	.576	.592	.642	.652	.567	.684	.667	.760	.712	.833	.900	.786	.800
4. Japan					**.526**	.504	.505	.564	.621	.587	.588	.554	.605	.705	.804	.708	.957	.957	.700	.857
5. France						**.504**	.512	.527	.531	.573	.512	.600	.547	.737	.735	.741	.900	.981	.667	.857
6. Mexico							**.500**	.553	.618	.660	.589	.609	.586	.744	.672	.672	.750	.882	.692	.889
7. Australia								**.507**	.624	.571	.544	.679	.570	.729	.746	.638	.600	.929	.688	.714
8. Brazil									**.557**	.545	.550	.561	.561	.656	.673	.698	.750	.911	.639	.800
9. Belgium										**.583**	.463	.595	.551	.545	.591	.548	.714	.889	.600	.857
10. Italy											**.524**	.515	.500	.703	.621	.531	.667	.909	.600	.667
11. Spain												**.500**	.522	.676	.725	.730	.667	.969	.667	.750
12. Netherlands													**.537**	.641	.750	.727	.969	.990	.571	.667
13. Colombia														**.700**	.677	.633	.500	.909	.444	.667
14. Argentina															**.700**	.529	.529	.600	.667	.857
15. S. Africa																**.583**	.900	.600	.667	.900
16. India																	**.500**	.900	.667	.900
17. Taiwan																		**.625**	.800	.667
18. Philippines																			**.667**	.850
19. Ireland																				**.850**
20. S. Korea																				**.900**

Notes

Chapter I

1. Vernon, R., "The Product Cycle Hypothesis in a New International Environment," *The Oxford Bulletin of Economics and Statistics* (forthcoming 1979); Dunning, J.H., "The Determinants of International Production," *Oxford Economic Papers,* November 1973; Dunning, J.H., and Buckley, P.J., "International Production and Alternative Models of Trade," University of Reading Discussion Papers in International Investment and Business Studies, No. 16, 1974; Parry, T.G., "Factors in the International Production of Multinational Enterprises," University of South Wales Discussion Paper No. 28, October 1977; Giddy, I.H., "The Demise of the Product Cycle Model in International Business Theory," *Columbia Journal of World Business,* Spring 1978, pp. 90-97.

2. This point is developed in Dubin, M., Foreign Acquisitions and the Spread of the Multinational Firm, unpublished doctoral dissertation, Harvard Business School, 1976.

3. Curhan, J.P.; Davidson, W.H.; and Rajan Suri, *Tracing the Multinationals* (Cambridge: Ballinger, 1977), p. 394.

4. The costs of uncertainty in unit cost and revenue estimates are developed in Dopuch, N., Birnberg, J.G., and Demski, J., "An Extension of Standard Cost Variance Analysis," *The Accounting Review,* July 1977, pp. 526-36. The international implications of this issue are developed in a Harvard Business School case: Chandler Home Products, ICCH No. 9-377-232, Harvard Business School, 1977.

5. For a review of basic location decision models, see Nugent, C.E., Vollman, T.E., and Ruml, J., "An Experimental Comparison of Techniques for the Assignment of Facilities to Locations," *Operations Research,* March 1968. A more recent work is Rosenthal, R.E., White, J.A., and Young, D., "Stochastic Dynamic Location Analysis," *Management Science,* February 1978, pp. 645-53. A study with special emphasis on international location decisions is Pomper, C.L., International Facilities Planning: An Integrated Approach, unpublished doctoral dissertation, Harvard Business School, 1974.

6. Aliber, R.Z., "A Theory of Direct Foreign Investment," in Kindleberger, C.P. (ed.), *The International Corporation* (Cambridge: MIT Press, 1970).

7. Grubel, H.G., "Internationally Diversified Portfolios: Welfare Gains and Capital Flows," *American Economic Review,* December 1968, pp. 1299-1314; Lessard, D.R., "International Portfolio Diversification: A Multivariate Analysis for a Group of Latin American Countries," *Journal of Finance,* June 1973; Solnik, B., "The International Pricing of Risk,"

Journal of Finance, May 1974, pp. 365-78; Rugman, A.M., "Risk Reduction by International Diversification," *Journal of International Business Studies,* Fall 1976.

8.   Data on average price-earnings ratios for 17 nations are presented monthly in *Capital International Perspectives* (Geneva: Capital International S.A.). These data show that average P-E ratios in the United States have declined substantially relative to average P-E's in other national security markets. From being at the top of the list through the 1960s, the U.S. has ranked very near the bottom of the list through most of the 1970s.

9.   Markowitz, H., *Portfolio Selection: Efficient Diversification of Investments* (New York: Wiley, 1959).

10.   See, however, Logue, D.E., and Rogalski, R.J., "Offshore Alphas: Should Diversification Begin at Home," *Journal of Portfolio Management,* Winter 1979.

11.   Hymer, S., *The International Operations of National Firms: A Study of Direct Foreign Investments* (Cambridge: MIT Press, 1976).

12.   Caves, R.E., "International Corporations: The Industrial Economics of Foreign Investment," *Economica,* February 1971, pp. 1-27.

13.   Vernon, R., "International Investment and International Trends in the Product Cycle," *Quarterly Journal of Economics,* May 1966, pp. 190-207.

14.   Chandler, A.D., *Strategy and Structure* (Cambridge: MIT Press, 1962).

15.   Dubin, M., *op. cit.*

16.   Buckley, P.J., and Casson, M.C., *The Future of the Multinational Enterprise* (New York: Holmes and Meier, 1976).

17.   Arrow, K.J., "Economic Welfare and the Allocation of Resources for Inventions" in National Bureau of Economic Research, *The Rate and Direction of Inventive Activity* (Princeton: Princeton University Press, 1962), p. 117.

18.   Preference theory is an integral component of Bayesian decision theory. For a simple introduction, see Hammond, J., "Better Decisions with Preference Theory," *Harvard Business Review,* November-December 1967. For a more detailed view, see Schlaifer, R.S., *Analysis of Decisions Under Uncertainty* (New York: McGraw-Hill, 1969); Hamburg, M., *Statistical Analysis for Decision Making* (New York: Harcourt Brace Jovanovich, 1977), pp. 575-87.

19.   The "defensive" model of foreign direct investment is developed in Stobaugh, R.B., "How Investment Abroad Creates Jobs at Home," *Harvard Business Review,* September-October 1972.

20.   Knight, F.M., *Risk, Uncertainty and Profit* (New York: Harper and Row, 1965).

21.   Vernon, R., *Sovereignty at Bay* (New York: Basic Books, 1971), p. 107.

22. Wells, L.T., Jr., *The Product Life Cycle and International Trade* (Boston: Division of Research, Harvard Business School, 1972), p. 26.

Chapter II

1. U.S. Department of Commerce, *Survey of Current Business*, "U.S. Balance of Payment Developments," March 1979.

2. U.S. Department of Commerce, *Survey of Current Business*, "Sales of Majority-owned Foreign Manufacturing Affiliates," February 1977.

3. U.S. Department of Commerce, *Survey of Current Business*, "U.S. International Transactions in Royalties and Fees," December 1973. National Science Board, *Science Indicators 1976* (Washington: Government Printing Office, 1977), pp. 30-33.

4. Dubin, M., *op. cit.*

5. For a discussion of various measures of market size, see Stobaugh, R.B., "Where in the World Should We Put that Plant?", *Harvard Business Review*, January-February 1969.

6. For a review of political risk and foreign investment, see Kobrin, S.J., "Political Risk: A Review and Reconsideration," Sloan School Working Paper, M.I.T., May 1978.

7. This topic is covered in Stobaugh, R.B., "How to Analyze Foreign Investment Climates," *Harvard Business Review*, September-October 1969.

8. Assuming that labor costs are the most significant determinants of production cost differentials, the U.S. has benefited over the last decade from slower wage increases. Unit labor costs in the U.K. and Canada, expressed in dollars (1967 = 100):

	1972	1977
U.K.	126.6	200.2
Canada	122.0	183.7
U.S.	118.1	168.3

From: U.S. Department of Commerce, *International Economic Indicators*, March 1979, p 86.

9. Linder, S.B., *Essays on Trade and Transformation* (New York: Wiley, 1962).

10. Vernon, R., *Storm Over the Multinationals* (Cambridge: Harvard University Press, 1977), Chap. 3.

11. Davidson, W.H., "Patterns of Factor-saving Innovation in the Industrialized World," *European Economic Review*, October 1976.

12. Gruber, W.M., and Marquis, D.G. (eds.), *Factors in the Transfer of Technology* (Cambridge: MIT Press, 1969); Rogers, E.M., and Shoemaker, F.F., *Communication of Innovations* (New York: Free Press, 1971).

13. Vaupel, J.W., Characteristics and Motivations of U.S. Corporations that Manufacture Abroad, unpublished manuscript, 1971.

14. For a presentation of this technique, see Kemeny, J.G., and J.L. Snell, *Mathematical Models in the Social Sciences* (Cambridge: MIT Press, 1962), Chapter II.

15. The assignment of values to Aij was performed in the following manner. Values are assigned in a 20 by 20 matrix of countries. If Canada was the first country in a parent-industry sequence, as in this case, each cell in the row for Canada is increased by one, because production for this parent-industry appeared in Canada before any other country. If the U.K. appears second, the values in the row for the U.K. are increased by one in all cells except that under the Canada column. Values are assigned in this manner for each nation in which production was initiated in 1976.

16. The concept of center-periphery expansion patterns has been broadly cited. See, for example, Lindblom, C.E., "The Science of 'Muddling Through' ", *Public Administration Review,* Spring 1959, pp. 79-88; Aharoni, Y., *The Foreign Investment Decision Process* (Boston: Division of Research, Harvard Business School, 1966), p. 50; Permutter, H.V., "Social Architectural Problems of the International Firm," *Quarterly Journal of AIESEC International* August 1967, pp. 33-44; Vernon, R., *Sovereignty at Bay* (New York: Basic Books, 1971), pp. 62-63; Wind, Y., Douglas, S.P., and Perlmutter, H.V., "Guidelines for Developing International Marketing Strategies," *Journal of Marketing* (April 1973), pp. 14-23; Johanson, J., and Vahlne, J.E., "Internationalization of the Firm," *Journal of International Business Studies,* Spring 1977, pp. 23-32; and Quinn, J.B., "Strategic Change: Logical Incrementalism," *Sloan Management Review,* Fall 1978, pp. 7-21.

17. These matrices were compiled through the use of a reference index which assigned each country-pair manufacturing observation into an Aij or Aji in one of the four matrices. For instance, in the example developed earlier, the row for Canada received an increment in each of the other 19 country columns. Now, each of these increments can go into only one of the four conditional matrices. To determine which of the four an increment will be posted to, the reference system determines the status of each country-pair as of the year production began in Canada. The reference index assigns either an N or P to Canada as of 1959 for the parent in question, and assigns an N or a P for each of the other 19 countries for 1959 for this parent. An N signifies that there was no prior production in the country as of 1959, a P that manufacturing was taking place by the parent in the country before 1959. The combination of these two variables determines the table in which each country-pair increment is recorded. If the U.K. appears second in the sequence, entering in 1963, the process continues for the U.K. with the base year 1963, and so on. It is important to note that Fij + Fji ≠ 1.0 in the PN and NP tables. As defined and discussed in Appendix II, FijPN + FjiNP = 1.0.

18. Teece, D.J., "Technology Transfer by Multinational Firms," *Economic Journal,* 1977.

19. This policy has been central to Japan's development strategy. A number of other nations have employed similar policies. See for example Balasubramanyamn, V.N., *International Transfer of Technology to India* (New York: Praeger, 1973); *Barlow Corporation in India,* ICCH No. 9-370-092, Harvard Business School, 1972; Furnish, D.B., "The Andean Common Market's Common Regime for Foreign Investments," in Sauvant, K.P. and Lavipour, F.G. (eds.), *Controlling Multinational Enterprises* (Boulder: Westview Press, 1976); G.K. Helleiner, "International Technology Issues: Southern Needs and Northern

Responses," in Bhagwati, J.N. (ed.), *The New International Economic Order: The North-South Debate* (Cambridge: MIT Press, 1977).

20. For documentation and discussion of the effects of rising global competition, see: Vernon, R. *Storm Over the Multinationals, op. cit.,* Chapter 4.

21. Hexner, E., *International Cartels* (Chapel Hill: University of North Carolina Press, 1946).

Chapter III

1. Chandler, A.D., *Strategy and Structure, op. cit.;* Chandler, A.D., *The Visible Hand* (Boston: Harvard University Press, 1977); Lawrence, P.R., and Lorsch, J.W., *Organization and Environment* (Boston: Division of Research, Harvard Business School, 1967); and Woodward, J., *Industrial Organization: Theory and Practice* (London: Oxford University Press, 1965).

2. Burns, T., and Stalker, G.M., *The Management of Innovation* (London: Tavistock, 1961); Chandler, A.D., *Strategy and Structure, op. cit.;* Galbraith, J.K., *Designing Complex Organizations* (Reading, Mass.: Addison-Wesley, 1973); Ouchi, W.G., "The Relationship between Organizational Structure and Organizational Control," *Administrative Science Quarterly,* March 1977, pp. 95-113; and "The Transmission of Control through Organizational Hierarchy," *Academy of Management Journal,* June 1978.

3. Perrow, C., *Organizational Analysis: A Sociological View* (Belmont, Calif.: Wadsworth, 1970); Greiner, L.E., "Patterns of Organizational Change," *Harvard Business Review,* May-June 1967.

4. March, J.G., and Simon, H., *Organizations* (New York: Wiley, 1958); Blau, P.M., and Scott, W.R., *Formal Organizations* (San Francisco: Chandler, 1962); and Galbraith, J.K., "Organizational Design: An Information Processing View" in Lorsch, J. W., and Lawrence, P.R. (eds.), *Organizational Planning* (Homewood, Ill.: Irwin, 1972).

5. This issue is addressed in Solomons, D., *Divisional Performance: Measurement and Control* (New York: Harper, 1965).

6. Lawrence, P.R., and Lorsch, J.W., *op. cit.*

7. These structures are described in Davis, S.M., "Trends in the Organization of Multinational Corporations," *Columbia Journal of World Business,* Summer 1976, pp. 59-71.

8. Baumol, W.J., *Business Behavior, Value and Growth* (New York: MacMillan, 1959); Cyert, R., and March, J.G., *A Behavioral Theory of the Firm* (Englewood Cliffs, N.J.: Prentice-Hall, 1963); Galbraith, J.K., *The New Industrial State* (Boston: Houghton Mifflin, 1967); Simon, H., *Administrative Behavior* (New York: Free Press, 1948); and Stevens, G.V.C., "The Determinants of Investment," in Dunning, J.M. (ed.), *Economic Analysis and the Multinational Enterprise* (London: Allen and Unwin, 1974).

Chapter IV

1. From Harvard Multinational Enterprise Project Surveys of the Fortune 500.

2. Vernon, R., and Davidson, W.H., *op. cit.,* p. 21.

3. Franko, L.G., *The European Multinationals* (London: Harper and Row, 1976).

4. Tsurumi, Y., *The Japanese are Coming* (Cambridge: Ballinger, 1976).

5. Wells, L.T., Jr., "The Internationalization of Firms from the Developing Countries," in Agmon, T., and Kindleberger, C.P. (eds.), *Multinationals from Small Countries* (Cambridge: MIT Press, 1976).

6. Vernon, R., "International Trade and Investment in the Product Life Cycle," *op. cit.*

7. Hymer, S., *The International Operations of National Firms, op. cit.*

8. Caves, R.E., "International Corporations: The Industrial Economics of Foreign Investment," *op. cit.*

9. Buckley, P.J., and Casson, M.C., *The Future of the Multinational Enterprise, op. cit.;* Tilton, J.E., *The Future of Nonfuel Minerals* (Washington, D.C.: The Brookings Institution, 1977).

10. Baranson, J., *The International Transfer of Automobile Technology to Developing Countries* (New York: UNITAR, 1971); Finan, W.F., *The International Transfer of Semiconductor Technology through U.S. Based Firms* (New York: National Bureau of Economic Research, 1975); Harman, A.J., *The International Computer Industry: Innovation and Comparative Advantage* (Cambridge: Harvard University Press, 1971); Hufbauer, G.C., *Synthetic Materials and the Theory of International Trade* (London: Duckworth, 1965); Jequier, N., "International Technology Transfer in the Telecommunications Industry," Germidis, D. (ed.), *Transfer of Technology by Multinational Corporations* (Paris: OECD, 1977), Vol. II; Stobaugh, R.B., *The International Transfer of Technology in the Establishment of the Petrochemical Industry in Developing Countries* (New York: UNITAR, 1971); and Tilton, J.E., *International Diffusion of Technology: The Case of Semiconductors* (Washington: Brookings Institution, 1971).

11. Maddala, G., and Knight, P., "International Diffusion of Technical Change: A Case Study of the Oxygen Steel Making Process," *Economic Journal,* September 1967, pp. 531-58; Nasbeth, L.E., and Ray, G.F., *The Diffusion of New Industrial Processes: An International Study* (Cambridge, U.K.: Cambridge University Press, 1974); Ray, G.F., "The Diffusion of New Technology: A Study of Ten Processes in Nine Industries," *National Institute Economic Review,* May 1969, pp. 40-83; and Botti, J.M., The International Diffusion of the Linz-Donau Converter, unpublished dissertation, Technische Hochschule, Vienna, 1973.

12. Leroy, G.P., Multinational Corporate Strategy: A Framework of Analysis of Worldwide Diffusion of Products, unpublished doctoral dissertation, University of California at Berkeley, 1974; and Stobaugh, R.B., and Curhan, J.P., *A Model Study of International Technology Transfer by Three Multinational Enterprises* (Washington: National Science Foundation, 1975).

13. Vernon, R., *Storm Over the Multinationals* (Cambridge: Harvard University Press, 1977), pp. 80-81.

14. The technological success of the Concorde and the commercial success of Airbus pose challenges to the U.S. aerospace industry. See Hearings before the Senate Subcommittee on International Finance, "Export Policy," March 20-21, April 7, 13, 1978 (Washington: Government Printing Office, 1978), Part IV.

15. The French Super Phenix Breeder Reactor, initiatives in fuel processing and recycling by EURODIF and URENCO, and generous export financing by foreign governments have virtually eliminated the once-substantial foreign market for the U.S. nuclear equipment industry. See Davidson, W.H., The International Nuclear Equipment Industry, Amos Tuck School, Dartmouth College, 1979; and Joskow, P.L., "The International Nuclear Industry Today: The End of the American Monopoly," *Foreign Affairs*, July 1976.

16. "France Elbows in on Worldwide U.S. Phone Sales," *World Business Weekly*, June 4, 1979, pp. 9-11.

17. "The TV-Set Competition that Won't Go Away," *Business Week*, May 8, 1978, p. 86; "Backing off Basics," *Wall Street Journal*, October 19, 1977, p. 36; and "Videodiscs to Market," *World Business Weekly*, March 12, 1979, p. 9-10.

18. Magee, S.P., *op. cit.*

19. Vernon, R., "The Location of Economic Activity," in Dunning, J.H. (ed.) *Economic Analysis and the Multinational Enterprise, op. cit.*

20. Stobaugh, R.B., "Utilizing Technical Know-how in a Foreign Investment and Licensing Program," *op. cit.*

21. Gruber, W.H., Mehta, D., and Vernon, R., "The R&D Factor in International Trade and International Investment of United States Industries," *Journal of Political Economy*, February 1967, pp. 20-38; and Keesing, D.B., "The Impact of Research and Development on United States Trade," *Journal of Political Economy*, February 1967, pp. 38-49.

22. Graham, E.M., Oligopolistic Imitation and European Direct Investment in the United States, unpublished doctoral dissertation, Harvard Business School, 1979.

23. This issue is discussed in Stopford, J.M., and Wells, L.T., Jr., *Managing the Multinational Enterprise* (New York: Basic Books, 1972), pp. 99, 119-24. Such considerations were critical in IBM's conflict with the Indian government. See Kleinfield, N.R., "IBM to leave India to Avoid Loss of Control," *New York Times*, November 16, 1977, p. D1; and "IBM Plans to End Indian Operations: Won't Comply with Government Orders," *Journal of Commerce*, November 1977, p. 8.

24. Stobaugh, R.B., "Utilizing Technical Know-how in a Foreign Investment and Licensing Program," *op. cit.*

25. Gruber, W.H., Mehta, D., and Vernon, R., "The R&D Factor in International Trade and International Investment of United States Industries," *op. cit.;* and Keesing, D.B., "The Impact of Research and Development on United States Trade," *op. cit.*

26.   Mansfield noted that "The extent of the uncertainty associated with using the innovation" is one of four factors governing speed of adoption. Mansfield, E., *The Economics of Technological Change* (New York: Norton, 1968).

Chapter V

1.   For a discussion of this issue, see Stevens, G.V.C., "The Determinants of Investment," in Dunning, J.H. (ed.) *Economic Analysis and the Multinational Enterprise, op. cit.*

2.   Several cases address this issue. See, for example Sigma Corporation in Italy (A&B) ICCH 4-337-085 and 4-337-086; See also Leroy, G.P., Multinational Corporate Strategy: A Framework of Analysis of Worldwide Diffusion of Products, unpublished doctoral dissertation, University of California at Berkeley, 1974; and Stobaugh, R.B., et al., *Nine Investments Abroad and Their Impact at Home* (Boston: Division of Research, Harvard Business School, 1977).

3.   This definition is developed in Stobaugh, R.B., "How Investment Abroad Creates Jobs at Home," *Harvard Business Review,* September-October 1972.

4.   Knight, F.M., *Risk, Uncertainty and Profit, op. cit.*

5.   Hammond, J., "Better Decisions with Preference Theory," *Harvard Business Review, op. cit.*

6.   The concept of risk premium is developed in Fisher, I., *The Rate of Interest* (New York: MacMillan 1970), p. 215; See also Hirschleifer, J., "Risk, the Discount Rate and Investment Decisions," *American Economic Review,* May 1961, pp. 112-30.

7.   This point is developed in Vernon, R., "The Location of Economic Activity," in Dunning, J.H. (ed.) *Economic Analysis and the Multinational Enterprise, op. cit.*

8.   Horst, T., "Firm and Industry Determinants of the Decision to Invest Abroad: An Empirical Study," *Review of Economics and Statistics,* August 1972.

9.   Telesio, P., Foreign Licensing Policy in Multinational Enterprises, unpublished doctoral dissertation, Harvard Business School, 1977.

10.   Stopford, J.M., and Wells, L.T., Jr., *Managing the Multinational Enterprise* (New York: Basic Books, 1972).

11.   Schumpeter, J.A., *The Theory of Economic Development* (Cambridge: Harvard University Press, 1934).

12.   Williamson, O.E., *Markets and Hierarchies: Analysis and Antitrust Implications* (New York: Free Press, 1975) Chap. 10.

13.   Chandler, A.P., *Strategy and Structure, op. cit.*

14. Sultan, R.G.M., *Pricing in the Electrical Oligopoly* (Boston: Division of Research, Harvard Business School, 1975).

15. On the System 370, see "Vincent Learson didn't Plan it that Way, but IBM's Toughest Competitor is IBM," *Fortune,* March 1972, p. 58. For the 4300, see "IBM 4300 Viewed Tough Act to Follow," *Computerworld,* March 19, 1979, p. 58; "IBM vs. IBM," *Datamation,* February 1979; and "IBM Seen Driving Firms from Computer Industry," *Computerworld,* February 19, 1979.

16. Stopford, J.M., and Wells, L.T., Jr., *Managing the Multinational Enterprise, op. cit.*

17. Knickerbocker, F.T., *Oligopolistic Research and Multinational Enterprise* (Boston: Division of Research, Harvard Business School, 1973).

Chapter VI

1. Schlaifer, R.S., *Analysis of Decisions Under Uncertainty, op. cit.;* and Hamburg, M., *Statistical Analysis for Decision Making, op. cit.,* pp. 588-624.

2. Hammond, J., "Better Decisions with Preference Theory," *op. cit.*

3. The growing literature on market failure includes Buckley, P.J., and Casson, M.C., *The Future of the Multinational Enterprise, op. cit.;* Magee, S.P., "Information and Multinational Corporation: An Appropriability Theory of Direct Foreign Investment," in Bhagwati, J. (ed.), *The New International Economic Order: The North-South Debate* (Cambridge: MIT Press, 1977); and Williamson, O.E., *Markets and Hierarchies: Analysis and Anti-trust Implications, op. cit.*

4. Dubin, M., *Foreign Acquisitions and the Spread of the Multinational Firm, op. cit.*

5. Leroy, G.P., Multinational Corporate Strategy: A Framework of Analysis of Worldwide Diffusion of Products, *op. cit.;* Hennart, J.-F., A Theory of Foreign Direct Investment, unpublished doctoral dissertation, University of Maryland, 1977; and Konz, L., Multinational Corporations and the International Transfer of Technology, unpublished doctoral dissertation, University of Texas at Dallas, 1976.

6. Giddy, I., "The Demise of the Product Cycle Model in International Business Theory," *op. cit.* As noted in Chapter I, over 90 percent of all foreign manufacturing subsidiaries realize the majority of their sales volume from the national market in which they are located. See figure I-1. As seen in Chapter II, the extension of U.S. product lines into foreign markets accounts for 65.0 percent and rising, of all foreign investment, based on product line observations. See Table 2-2.

7. See Notes 21 and 22 for Chapter I of this study for quotations to this effect.

8. This is in fact the approach developed in Vernon, R., "The Product Cycle Hypothesis in a New International Environment," *op. cit.*

9. An interesting view of this phenomena is described in Morris, M., Lavipour, F.G., and Savant, K.P., "The Politics of Nationalization: Guyana vs. Alcan" in Savant and Lavipour

(eds.) *Controlling Multinational Enterprises* (Boulder: Westview, 1976). See also Smith, D.N., and Wells, L.T., Jr., *Negotiating Third-World Mineral Agreements: Promises as Prologue* (Cambridge: Ballinger, 1975).

10.   Walters, K.D., and Monsen, R.J., "State-owned Business Abroad: New Competitive Threat," *Harvard Business Review,* March-April 1979.

11.   Tornedon, R.L., *Foreign Divestment by U.S. Multinational Corporations* (New York: Praeger, 1977).

12.   Rose, S., "Why the Multinational Tide is Ebbing," *Fortune, op. cit.* From Harvard Multinational Enterprise Project surveys of the Fortune 500.

13.   Franko, L.G., "Multinationals: The End of U.S. Dominance?", *op. cit.;* and Rose, S., "Why the Multinational Tide is Ebbing," *op. cit.*

14.   U.S. Department of Commerce, *Survey of Current Business,* January 1967, p. 27 and August 1976, p. 42.

15.   Curhan, J.P.; Davidson, W.H.; and Rajan Suri, *Tracing the Multinationals, op. cit.*

16.   "R&D is Losing its High Priority," *Business Week,* May 12, 1973, p. 198; *Science Indicators* (Washington: Government Printing Office, 1977), pp. 46-48; and "Survey of Corporate Research and Development Spending," 1975-78, Annual, *Business Week.*

17.   "Backing off Basics," *Wall Street Journal,* October 18, 1977, p. 1.

18.   Wiesner, J., "Has the U.S. Lost its Initiative in Technological Innovation?" *Technology Review,* July-August, 1976; "The Breakdown of U.S. Innovation," *Business Week,* February 16, 1976, p. 56; and *Science Indicators* (Washington: Government Printing Office, 1977), pp. 20-30.

19.   Table 2-2 in Chapter II reveals that the introduction of additional product lines into existing subsidiaries accounted for less than 10 percent of all foreign investment activity in 1961-65, but 44.1 percent of all activity between 1971-75.

20.   The importance of foreign returns in financing R&D projects is developed in Mansfield, E., Romeo, A., and Wagner, S. "Foreign Trade and U.S. Research and Development," paper presented at the American Economic Association Conference held in Chicago, August 30, 1978.

21.   See "Using PIMS and Portfolio Analyses in Strategic Market Planning: A Comparative Analysis," Harvard Business School Case, ICCH Number 9-578-017.

22.   Bagnall, W.R., *Samuel Slater and the Early Development of Cotton Manufacture in the United States* (Middletown, Conn.: J.S. Stewart, 1890).

23.   Servan-Schreiber, J.J., *The American Challenge* (New York: Atheneum, 1968).

24.   Helleiner, G.K., "The Rate of Multinational Corporations in the Less Developed Countries Trade in Technology," *World Development,* April 1975, pp. 161-89; Lall, S., and Streeten,

P., *Foreign Investment, Transnationals and Developing Countries* (Boulder: Westview Press, 1977).

25. Chudson, W.A., "Multinational Enterprises in Developing Countries: Some Issues in the Manufacturing Sector" in Boarman, P.M., and Schollhammer, H., *Multinational Corporations and Governments* (New York: Praeger, 1975).

26. Viewpoints supporting of the labor point of view can be found in Musgrave, P.B., *Direct Investment Abroad and Multinationals: Effects on the U.S. Economy* (Washington: Government Printing Office, 1975); Thurow, L.C., "International Factor Movements and the American Distribution of Income," *Intermountain Economic Review*, Spring 1976, pp. 13-25; and Frank, R.M., and Freeman, R.T., *Multinational Corporations and Domestic Employment*, (Washington: U.S. Department of Labor, 1975).

27. Goldfinger, N., "The Case for Burke-Hartke," *Columbia Journal of World Business*, Summer 1972.

28. Stobaugh, R.B., "How Investment Abroad Creates Jobs at Home," *op. cit.;* Stobaugh, R.B., et al., *Nine Investments Abroad and Their Impact at Home* (Boston: Division of Research, Harvard Business School, 1976).

29. Hufbauer, G.C., and Adler, F.M., *Overseas Manufacturing Investment and the Balance of Payments* (Washington: U.S. Treasury Department, 1968); and Piekarz, R.R., *The Effects of International Technology Transfer on the U.S. Economy* (Washington: National Science Foundation, 1974).

30. See "Europe Courts Ford," *World Business Weekly*, March 5, 1979, pp. 9-10.

31. One of the most notable cases concerns U.S. intervention in a decision by Michelin Tire Company to establish a plant in Canada to serve the U.S. tire market. See "Michelin Tire Manufacturing Company of Canada Ltd." Harvard Business School Case, ICCH Number 9-378-668.

32. The implications of this prospect are discussed in Vernon, R., *Storm Over the Multinationals, op. cit.*, Chaps. 8-9.

Appendix II

1. Curhan, J.P.; Davidson, W.H.; and Rajan Suri, *Tracing the Multinationals* (Cambridge: Ballinger, 1977).

2. See also Vernon, R., and Davidson, W.H., *Foreign Production of Technology-intensive Products by U.S.-based Multinational Enterprises* (Washington, D.C.: National Science Foundation, 1979).

Index